The
Afternoon Hiker

THE Afternoon HIKER

A GUIDE TO CASUAL HIKES IN THE GREAT SMOKY MOUNTAINS

J.L. and Lin Stepp

MOUNTAIN HILL PRESS

Mountain Hill Press

a division of S & S Communications

The Afternoon Hiker
Copyright @ 2014
James L. Stepp

Cover Design by Elizabeth Wright
Cover photo by J.L. Stepp.
Interior photos by J.L and Lin Stepp
Hand-drawn original art by Lin M. Stepp
Trail narratives by J.L. and Lin Stepp
Editorial Assistance by Sherry Lewis

Published by Mountain Hill Press
a division of S & S Communications

Author note. This is a non-fiction guidebook created by the authors based on their hiking experiences in the Great Smoky Mountains National Park area. Effort has been made to ensure accuracy of specific environs and place names, but places and names change over time as do descriptive trail details.

Library of Congress Cataloging-in-Publication Data

Stepp, J.L. and Lin
 The Afternoon Hiker: A Guide to Casual Hikes in the Great Smoky Mountains
 by J.L. and Lin Stepp
 ISBN 978-0-692-02046-3

Non-Fiction. 1. Hiking—Tennessee—Guidebooks. 2. Trails—Tennessee—Guidebooks.
 3. Tennessee—Guidebooks.
 I. Stepp, J.L. and Lin   II. Title
 Library of Congress Control Number: 2013921632

DEDICATION

This book is dedicated to our son Max Stepp—who has always loved the outdoors and the Smoky Mountains and enjoys hiking with us whenever he is in Tennessee.

ACKNOWLEDGMENTS

Thanks and gratitude to the many organizations and groups that helped to create and continue to maintain the wonderful hiking trails in the Great Smoky Mountains National Park:

- The Great Smoky Mountains National Park Service that maintains all the national park trails and, along with their many volunteers who work through the Adopt-A-Trail Program and the Volunteers In Park (VIP) organizations, helps to keep trails clear and accessible, picks up trash, trims shrubs or trees that encroach on the trails, and restores and maintains historic sites.

- The Friends of the Smokies organization that enables programs such as Trails Forever and aids the Great Smoky Mountains National Park Service in maintaining the trails.

- The Smoky Mountains Hiking Club, whose Appalachian Trail Volunteers maintain all sections of the Appalachian Trail in the park.

Thanks also to our daughter Katherine Stepp, who contributed her graphics skills to help with format and layout design of this book and who created and maintains our joint author website at: *www.linstepp.com*

Final thanks to the Lord for the beauty of this earth and for the privilege to enjoy it.

TABLE OF CONTENTS

Note from authors J.L. and Lin Stepp...
The trails in this book are written in the chronological order in which we walked and explored them, making this guidebook a unique memoir of our journey of discovery in the Great Smoky Mountains National Park. At the end of the guidebook are an Alphabetical Trail Index and a Trail Index by Regions to help hikers locate any specific trail of interest by two alternate methods.
"Happy Trails to you until we meet again." - Roy Rogers

About the Trail Mileage:
The full mileage was not hiked on every trail in this book. Only parts of longer trails were hiked so that the average hiking distance of all trails would average 5-8 miles roundtrip—a good distance for an "afternoon hike."

About the Directions to the Trails:
We provided directions to the trails in this guidebook coming from outside the national park, beginning from the Knoxville, Tennessee, side of the Smokies where we live. If entering the park from another city or state, simply pick up on the trail directions from a closer point as the provided directions move closer to the trailhead. You can easily adapt the directional information by looking at a highway map or trails map of the area.

On the Cooper Road Trail at Abrams Campground

Smoky Mountain Novels
by Lin Stepp

SECOND HAND ROSE
DELIA'S PLACE
FOR SIX GOOD REASONS
TELL ME ABOUT ORCHARD HOLLOW
THE FOSTER GIRLS

And coming soon ... DOWN BY THE RIVER
Website: *www.linstepp.com*

Tennessee Fishing & Hunting Guide Magazine
by J.L. Stepp

Printed Monthly
Or Online at: *www.tnfhg.com*

Introduction

We titled this hiking guide *The Afternoon Hiker* because the hikes described within are just that: hikes that can easily be accessed and completed in an afternoon by average people. We began our hikes of the Smokies in the mid 1990s and like most newcomers to the hiking sport we held a few misconceptions. First of all, we thought we couldn't be "real" hikers because we weren't in super physical shape and because we were working middle-aged people who usually only had weekends to do such activities. Secondly, we envisioned hikes in the Smokies as long-distance treks for Sierra-club types laden with backpacks and gear. We were wrong on both counts! Sure, the first few hikes we experienced some aching and tired muscles but our stamina and strength soon increased with the hiking and we found we could manage any trail. We also discovered that there were hundreds of trails in the Smokies that were easily accessable and a satisfying portion of each could be hiked in an afternoon without an overnight campout and marathon. So, two middle-aged workers discovered the joy of hiking on weekends and the wonder of the mountains.

We carried our camera on each hike and chronicled each trail description to have a journal and scrapbook of photos and fond memories of the hikes and variety the mountains offered. This was at first just for our own enjoyment of remembering our hiking experiences. It was sometime later that we toyed with the idea of putting these trail photos and descriptions in a book. We had two main motivations. First, we found that some hiking books we read contained not only trail descriptions, but sometimes lots of other information such as histories, biographical sketches, geographic and topographic facts, and non-trail related topics. Secondly, we realized many of these hiking books were written from the perspective of long, strenuous loop-hikes or overnight treks for veteran (or younger) hikers and failed to give adequate descriptions of the earliest portions of the trails most day hikers would walk.

So we decided to produce a fun hiking book with just the trail facts and no superfluous information. We tried to describe each trail as accurately and honestly as we could from the perspective of average weekend hikers. We also wanted to include many of our trail photos to both entice the reader and make the book more fun. Our desire is that we can encourage and motivate more people to experience the healthy joy of hiking the Smokies. Our message is this: you can experience the fun of mountain hiking even if you are middle-aged (or older), working full time or less, and by simply being in reasonable health for outdoor walking without being a workout freak. Many hikes have mild ascents and even on steeper trails you can look forward to an easier downhill return hike. Anyone in fair health can start with easier, shorter hikes and take on more strenuous hikes as the body gets conditioned—and it will. You will be amazed at how quickly the body strengthens through hiking and how easily the mind and soul relax in the beauty of the Smoky Mountains. Hope to see you soon on the trail!

Lin & J.L. Stepp

Middle Prong Trail

Date Hiked: SUMMER - July 6th
Mileage: 4.6 miles Roundtrip
Our Rating: Moderate
Directions: Hwy 321 to Townsend Wye; Right on Laurel Creek Road; left at 0.2 mile onto Tremont Road; drive 5.4 miles to road's end and parking; trail starts at gate.

Trail Description:

Lynn Camp Cascades

This was our first "official" hike as we started our exploration of the Smoky Mountains and began our hiking journal. We recommend this trail as an enjoyable first hike for anyone. The trail starts at the very end of the Tremont Road and follows along the banks of one of the Smokies' wide, tumbling streams.

The Middle Prong Trail begins by crossing a high, wooden bridge over Lynn Camp Prong. Below, the creek rushes downhill into the Middle Prong stream, making a pretty sight. The walking path beyond the bridge is an old logging roadbed, and hikers can walk side by side here, since the trail remains broad for several miles. After a gentle, gradual ascent through the woods, the trail arrives at Lynn Camp Cascades at approximately one half mile, where a series of plummeting waterfalls and tiered cascades spill over a succession of high rock shelves in the stream. Where the cascades begin sits a rustic log bench to rest on, one of many along the early part of this trail.

As you hike on, be sure to stop at the lookout boulder at the top of

the cascades where you'll enjoy another view back down the falls. Also, shortly after leaving the falls, watch for a side trail off to the left that leads down to a small, picturesque waterfall with a deep pool below it. This trail offers many memorable spots, and the ongoing Middle Prong Trail continues to be a broad and pleasant one to amble along as it winds gradually up

8

the valley between Timber and Green Camp ridges. To the left of the trail, the creek is a constant delight throughout this hike, with its rushing waters, giant boulders, shining falls and swirling cascades.

Besides the delights of the stream, this hiking trail is also known for its variety of wildflowers in spring and summer. On our later July hike, we saw black-eyed susans, wood asters, rhododendron, and galax spikes, and we enjoyed following a short side trail off the main path at 2.1 miles to an old, rusted car, a remnant of the old logging community that once existed in this Townsend community.

At 2.3 miles stands a sign for Panther Creek Trail on the left, the turn around for our first 4.6 miles round-trip hike. You can sit on the large boulders here by the streamside to rest before starting back. Just across the stream, you can see Panther Creek Trail starting up the hillside. The trail is named for wild panthers that once roamed the Smoky Mountains. Although no bridge spans the stream, when the water is down you can take off your boots and wade to the trail on the other side. Be careful if you try this. The knee-deep stream is swift and the rocks underwater slippery, making the crossing challenging.

If you decide to cross and extend your hike, which we did at a later date, you will find the ongoing trail climbs 2.2 miles sharply up the southwest flank of Blanket Mountain to Jakes Gap high above. The continuing pathway soon meets its namesake, Panther Creek, at about a half mile. The trail proceeds to crisscross several times over "hop-rocks," or rocks protruding above the water in the stream, as the climb continues. Some of these crossings may prove difficult, especially in the first mile of the trail. The path is steep but pretty, winding through many tun-

nels of rhododendron on the way to the gap and gaining almost 1,500 feet in the journey. Hiking the full distance to the end of Panther Creek to its intersection with Jakes Creek Trail and Miry Ridge Trail would extend your day hike to a 9-miles trip, a nice length for a veteran hiker but not for a beginner.

9

Metcalf Bottoms and Little

Date Hiked: SUMMER - July 13th
Mileage: 5.5 miles Roundtrip
Our Rating: Moderate
Directions: Hwy 321 to Townsend Wye; left on Little River Road to Metcalf Bottoms parking lot; trailhead on right just across the bridge over river.

Trail Description:

This is an interesting second hike to take in the Smokies. The trail begins just behind the Metcalf Bottoms picnic grounds. Park your car just

inside the picnic grounds entry road by the creek, walk over the bridge, and then look for the trail beginning on the immediate right. The 5.5 miles roundtrip hike, which begins here, takes you meandering by streams and woods to a historic one-room schoolhouse and then on to a restored pioneer homesite.

The Metcalf Bottoms Trail, leading to the school, starts just after crossing the Little River bridge. Turn right behind the park gate and follow the trail alongside the river. At approximately 0.2 mile, the trail turns left away from the stream to start up the hillside, passing a water tower and heading into the woods. As you follow the trail, you climb through hardwoods and then through a section of thick rhododendron as the path winds up and over a ridgeline. After a downhill walk, you emerge into an open and sunny streamside meadow. As the trail ends, the pathway crosses

Historic One-Room Schoolhouse

over the stream on a narrow footbridge to arrive at the log school. You can go inside to explore before hiking on. This one-room schoolhouse, complete with original student desks and blackboard, was built in 1882 and served its community for fifty-four years. Behind a weathered fence on a slope beside

Brier Gap

the school lies Greenbrier Cemetery, half of its stone markers the graves of children.

After leaving the school, walk through its small parking lot and turn right on Little Brier Gap Trail, an old settlers' roadbed that thins to a single-file pathway as it climbs the side of Little Mountain. The lower portion of the dirt road winds gently through an open woods among summer wildflowers, skirting alongside Brier Branch. Wide enough for cars to drive on, the first mile seems almost flat in comparison to most Smokies hikes. The last half-mile grows steeper and narrower as it climbs to a junction called Little Brier Gap. Here several trails intersect in an open crossroads. Little Greenbrier Trail swings right, Roundtop Trail turns left, and the ongoing unmarked trail follows a steep path down the back-side of Cove Mountain where it meets a side road in the valley below. At the intersection, felled logs provide a seat to rest on before starting the trip back.

On your return hike, watch for a sign on the left leading down a side trail to the Walker sisters' cabin. Be sure to walk the extra half-mile round trip to this historic site. The park has preserved a complete pioneer homestead here where

the five Walker sisters lived until the 1960s, thirty years after the park formed in 1934. A cabin, barn, and springhouse still stand on the grounds. Hikers can walk through the cabin rooms, look into the outbuildings, and then sit out on the cabin's porch steps, imagining early life as a pioneer in the Smokies. We always like to have our lunch here on the Walker cabin porch. It's a quiet and peaceful place.

When you hike the Metcalf Bottoms and Little Brier Gap trails, plan to bring along a cooler and picnic supplies, some charcoal and lawn chairs for later on. You can relax in the Metcalf Bottoms picnic grounds after your hike, wade in the creek, and cook hotdogs and marshmallows before you call it a day.

11

Alum Cave Trail

Date Hiked: SUMMER - July 20th
Mileage: 5 miles Roundtrip
Our Rating: Easy (1st part) - Strenuous (2nd Part)
Directions: Hwy 441 through Pigeon Forge; right over the Gatlinburg bypass; right up Newfound Gap Road. The Alum Cave Trail parking lots are on the left about 9 miles up from the Sugarlands Visitor Center.

Trail Description:

Lin with her parents - Phil & Joy Mathews

The Alum Cave Trail begins at a high elevation point in the Smokies and is a popular trail with tourists and locals. At Newfound Gap Road it starts to weave alongside Walker Camp Prong and Alum Cave Creek to Arch Rock. Then it climbs more steeply up the back-side of Mount Le Conte to reach the Alum Cave Bluffs.

The first mile and a half section of the trail, almost flat, travels through a cool, deep woods, passing among dense thickets of rhododendron along the stream. The path is soft underfoot, but you need to watch carefully for exposed tree roots. The hiking trail crosses the Walker Camp Prong and Alum Cave Creek on several scenic, man-made bridges. It's a joy to stop on these bridges, lean on the rails, and watch the mountain water splashing over boulders and rocks as it rushes noisily down the mountainside. If you catch the Alum Cave Trail at the right weeks in July, with the rhododendron in full bloom, it is incredibly beautiful. The rhododendron crowd the trail and cover the hills along the streams with a constant show of white and pink-tinged blooms. We have walked this trail with the rhododendron so thick and beautiful that people can hardly hike or walk for stopping to stare every few yards.

This trail is a favorite one for children and adults alike. At many points along the stream you can rock-hop on the big boulders in the stream, wade in the cold water, or spread a picnic lunch out on a flat rock. The trail does not begin to climb steeply until it gets to Arch Rock at 1.5 miles. At Arch Rock weathering has provided a crack and tunnel pathway through a huge rock boulder. Stone steps have been created through the boulder to the continuation of the hiking trail above. This is a great photo-shoot spot. Past Arch Rock, the path begins to wind away from the stream and climb steeply up the back-side of Mount Le Conte to Peregrine Peak and Alum Cave Bluffs. The upper trail grows more narrow, winding around the ridgelines, with several nice vistas along the way. One, at a rocky turning in the trail, is called Inspiration Point and looks out over the valley far below.

There is no actual cave at the Alum Cave Bluffs. There are just unusual alum and sandstone layers of rock on the mountaintop. These sandstone layers rise up from the mountain to create an overhanging bluff about 100 feet high. This is an interesting geological end-point to your hike, and there are some fine views of the Mount Le Conte summit and the peaks around it from this point at 5,000 feet. The Bluffs are a nice place at which to rest and have a picnic lunch before you start back down the mountain. The resident birds and little red squirrels, or "boomers," will help you finish up your lunch scraps.

From the Alum Cave Bluffs, you are halfway to Mount Le Conte. If you want to explore further before turning back, you can hike on up the trail less than a half mile more to a rocky ridge called Gracies Pulpit. Here you can get a fine view of four of the high Smokies peaks that are a

part of Mount Le Conte. And you'll find that the return hike from the Alum Cave Bluffs, being all downhill, is much easier than the hike in.

13

Andrews Bald or Forney

Date Hiked: SUMMER - July 27th
Mileage: 4 miles Roundtrip
Our Rating: Strenuous
Directions: Hwy 441 through Pigeon Forge; right over the Gatlinburg bypass, and right up Newfound Gap Road to top of mountain (Newfound Gap); then turn right on Clingmans Dome Road and follow it to the end of the parking lot.

Trail Description:

Andrews Bald is another well known and popular hike in the Smoky Mountains. The trail leads down to an open grassy bald on top of one of the highest mountains in the national park. The hike begins out of the back of the parking lot at Clingmans Dome Road where several other hikes begin as well. Look for the trail signs out of the lower left end of the parking lot for Forney Ridge Trail and Andrews Bald. Stay left at any trail junctions along the way.

The first mile of the trail moves downhill on a rocky, open slope, of-

fering little shade or relief from the heat on a hot, midsummer day. This early part of the trail seemed to wind in and out of old, shaly creek beds, often trekking through water or mud. We had to walk slowly and watch our feet carefully on this steep downhill trudge because of the loose rocks and mud slicks. Scraggly blackberry and blueberry bushes spread their stickery branches into the trail, creating an additional hazard. Clambering down this steep, open hillside with its challenging obstacles did not create happy memories.

At about 1.1 miles, the trail splits. The Forney Creek Trail takes off to the right and the Forney Ridge Trail turns to the left, leading on to Andrews Bald. Stay left at this intersection and continue to follow the Forney Ridge Trail, which becomes a more pleasant trail section than the previous mile. The pathway now winds through a predominantly fir and spruce forest with lush green fern and a variety

14

Ridge Trail

of mosses along the trail. Wildflowers dot the forest here in July, including sweeps of delicate bluets spreading alongside the trail. If you look closely, you may see some rare corn lillies, or skunk cabbage, with their greenish yellow flowers. At one point, we saw evidence of a previous fire with several blackened tree trunks alongside the path, and we spotted many felled and dead trees killed by the chestnut blight.

The downhill walk throughout this section of the trail is more gradual in descent and more appealing. However, we ran into some very muddy, boggy spots in this wooded area, often awkward to get around. On the July day we hiked, we also encountered many other hikers on the trail.

Toward the end of the hiking trail, the path rises up sharply and then drops downward, opening out from the forest to reach the beginning of the bald at 2.3 miles. No one is really sure what created the few grassy, open balds on several of the Smokies mountaintops, but Andrews Bald, originally called Anders Bald, is the largest and the highest in the Smoky Mountains at 5,860 feet. It is known for Catawba rhododendron and flame azaleas in early summer and for stunning views out across the mountains. We unfortunately saw neither of these the day we hiked. It was hot and hazy; there were no flowers and the views were obscured. The summer grasses and weeds on the bald were knee high, and the gnats and bugs were profuse on this muggy, July day. This made our plans to picnic on top of the bald unappealing. Instead, we hiked back into the shade of the woods to have a lunch on a fallen log before starting our hike back.

Awesome views of the mountains from the bald

The return hike to Clingmans Dome Road was harder than the hike in, since it was all uphill.

Little River Trail

Date Hiked: SUMMER - August 19th
Mileage: 6 miles Roundtrip
Our Rating: Easy
Directions: Hwy 441 through Gatlinburg to Sugarlands Visitor Center; turn right on Little River Road; after 4.9 miles turn left at the entrance to Elkmont; drive approximately 1.5 miles to trail signs just before campground entrance and turn left at signs; drive 0.6 mile up road to parking area for the trailhead.

Trail Description:

Little River Trail is one of our favorite hiking trails in the Smokies. It is an easy trail running alongside a beautiful and riotous mountain stream. The trail is a comfortable one for young and old. When you have friends or relatives visiting from out of state, this is a good trail to take them on.

The trail begins on a side road through an aging group of summer resort houses in the Elkmont area. The properties are tumbling down now, but they were once beautiful summer homes and well-maintained by family owners that still enjoyed them until the park took the properties. Many of these homes were

built by logging executives in the early 1900s. Elkmont was an active 86,000 acre logging camp in the late 1800s to early 1900s, and there are many bits of evidence of these logging activities to discover along the trail. As the early walk past some of the remaining summer houses ends, the trail moves toward the creek on a soft-footed dirt road. This pleasant road will follow up the Little River Trail in a pleasant, gradual ascent. The trail is broad, and you can easily walk in twos, or a group, and chat along the way.

The mountain stream on the left of the trail is the size of a small river, filled with deep pools, smooth boulders, tumbling cascades, and rushing falls. In many places large trees drape the banks of the stream and the trailside, making the pathway cool and shady. In other areas the trail widens out to ramble

alongside sunny fields, full of colorful wild flowers from spring through fall. It is not uncommon to see hikers walking the Little River Trail in the spring carrying a guidebook to wildflowers. The area is especially beautiful in April with blooms of trillium, mayapples, bee balm, violets, showy orchis, phlox, and many other mountain flowers at their peak.

There are many interesting large boulders and rocks along the hillsides and trail including a variety of lush ferns. In many places, the ferns and trees seem to grow right out of the rock crevices. Occasionally, the trail gets a little rocky

as it ascends gradually upward, but it is predominantly flat and comfortable underfoot. Along the pathway are many scenic spots at which to enjoy Little River's falls and cascades. There are big, flat rest rocks and several man-made benches along the trail, too—all nice for resting or picnicking. The first bench is at about one-half mile up the trail; the last is at 1.3 miles at the Cucumber Gap Trail intersection.

After the Cucumber Gap intersection, the trail narrows, climbing away from the stream and then returning to cross it on a wide, plank bridge. In spring, there are sweeps of purple phlox and trillium in this section of the trail. The pathway enters a more wooded section now and arrives

at the Huskey Gap Trail intersection at 1.7 miles. You may see mushrooms and ramps growing along the shaded trailside here, if you look carefully. At 2.7 miles, the trail crosses a second bridge, passes the Goshen Prong Trail intersection, and then just after the 3 miles point, crosses a third bridge. The river splits here to form an island between the streams. This is a scenic spot. We poked around here for a while and had our picnic on the island before turning around to start our hike back. Little River Trail continues on for two miles further, but for a nice day hike, turning around at the island gives you a 6 miles roundtrip hike.

Anthony Creek Trail

Date Hiked: SUMMER - August 31st
Mileage: 5.6 miles Roundtrip
Our Rating: Moderate - Strenuous
Directions: Take 321 into Townsend, following straight to T intersection, called the Wye, to right on Laurel Creek Road to the Cades Cove Picnic Grounds sign; turn left across the bridge and left again into the picnic area; follow road to back to the trailhead.
Trail Description:

This trail originates at the back right end of the Cades Cove picnic grounds. It is a crowded area on summer weekends and, especially, on holidays. Parking and access to the trail from the back of the parking lot is often difficult.

The trail is a somewhat rocky roadbed trail that rises gradually up the northwest side of Thunderhead Mountain from out of the picnic grounds. It follows the creek and is deeply shaded and scenic. Several log bridges criss-cross Anthony Creek as you hike this trail, giving you many views of this nice stream. The water level was down when we hiked, but there were still pretty little falls and rushing water tumbling over the rocks at these crossings. Fallen trees and rocks are heavily moss covered on this trail, due to the deep shade here. There were also many large mushrooms the day we hiked and an interesting variety of fungi/lichens growing up the trees. The Cades Cove area often catches heavy rainfall promoting this undercover lushness.

Anthony Creek is both a horse and a hiking trail, and it passes the Cades Cove horse camp early along its way. There are picnic tables by the stream here that are nice for hikers whenever the horse camp is not full. This is a popular horse trail, and as a hiker, you have to watch carefully for horse-piles on trails also shared by horses. Horses, also, often rough-up a trail and make it rockier and harder to walk on. And you will find Anthony Creek is a very rocky trail under foot—so you should wear thick-soled shoes or boots to hike it.

There are five stream crossings as you weave in and out over Anthony Creek on this 2.8 miles hike. The first of these, at 0.5 mile, is at a broad wooden

18

roadbridge over pretty cascades, but most of the other crossings are footlogs or rock-hop crossings. It is fun criss-crossing back and forth over the creek on this trail, and none of the crossings are hard to navigate. Anthony Creek Trail is a deep forest trail for the most part, and there are many hardwoods and evergreens overhead. Even on a hot day, it is shady and cool. However, by the time you have walked in a few miles, you are climbing more steeply and will work up a sweat regardless of the weather.

    The second and third creek crossings are at 0.8 mile and 1 mile. After the second bridge at 1 mile, the trail climbs more steeply than before until it reaches a fourth crossing and the Russell Field Trail intersection. There is a broad open area at this trail junction, and you will find a nice rock to rest on. The Anthony Creek Trail continues left here, becoming more narrow as it climbs on. Watch for a nice waterfall along the path at about 2 miles and, if you are hiking in July, you will see

many pretty rhododendron in this section of the trail. A little further on, look for large tulip trees and a huge hemlock growing right out of a rock. Campsite #9 at 2.8 miles is a good spot for a lunch break before starting the easier downhill hike back.

    Anthony Creek continues on for 0.7 mile further to meet the Bote Mountain Trail. Many seasoned hikers use this route to get to Spence Field, a high mountain meadow with spectacular views. The field is just above the junction of Bote Mountain on the Appalachian Trail. The hike up Anthony Creek and on to Spence Field is approximately 10.5 miles roundtrip.

Abrams Falls Trail

Date Hiked: FALL - September 7th
Mileage: 5 miles Roundtrip
Our Rating: Moderate
Directions: Take 321 to Townsend Wye, right on Laurel Creek Road to the Cades Cove entrance; follow Cades Cove Loop Rd 4.5 miles to gravel road on right to trailhead.

Trail Description:

Abrams Falls is one of those well known Smokies trails that almost everyone who visits the area hikes. It starts out of the Cades Cove, a popular tourist area, and the trail's scenic two and a half mile walk leads in to a beautiful waterfall.

Getting to the trailhead of Abrams Falls on the Cades Cove Loop often takes some time. Creeping traffic and groups of bikers slow the movement of traffic around the 11 miles scenic Cades Cove Loop. Often when tourists sight wildlife, like deer or a bear, or want to enjoy the scenery or take a photo, they simply stop their cars in the middle of the road to do so. Most seldom bother to pull over to the side of the road so that other traffic can pass on by. Because of this, the traffic movement often comes to a virtual stand-still in the Cove. So bring your patience with you for the drive to the trailhead, especially if you plan to hike to Abrams Falls on a busy weekend or a holiday.

The Abrams Falls Trail begins through a short woods walk to a bridge crossing over Abrams Creek. Follow the marked signs here as several other trails and walks branch out of this same area. The Abrams trail is a broad, pleasant, and soft-footed path, easy to walk on. It meanders through the woods and along Abrams Creek to the falls with many scenic stopping points on the creek along the way. The trail, moderate overall, has roller coaster ups and downs which may yield sore calves the next day if you do not hike often.

The trail crisscrosses the creek a few times on nice footbridges and there are several places along the path where you can walk out onto rocks by the stream to wade or to just enjoy a rest by the water. The first half mile of the trail is flat but then begins to climb above the creek. At about 1 mile, you top the first ridgeline, Arbutus Ridge, before the trail drops again back down to the creek. The walk winds pleasantly in and out of a pretty forest of hardwoods and evergreens. At approximately 1.8 miles you will rise up to Stony Ridge and then down again to the Wilson Creek footbridge. At 2.5 miles a sign directs hikers left down a steep side path and then left over another footbridge to the rocky path leading to the base of the falls.

Abrams Falls is a picture-perfect 20 foot plume falls spilling over a high ledge into a beautiful round pool below. There are usually many people here on a sunny day picnicking and enjoying the beauty of the falls. You can rock-hop up to the base of the waterfall or wade your feet in the cold mountain water. Occasionally, you will see people swimming in the pool below the falls, but we don't advise this. There have been drownings here. There have also been fatal accidents from people trying to climb up the rocks to the top of the falls. Our advice is to enjoy the falls from below—and to bring your camera for lots of pictures.

When you return from your hike and start back up the Cades Cove Loop Road in your car, watch for the turning into the Cades Cove Visitor Center and Museum and the Cable Mill historic area. If you're new to the Cades Cove area, it's fun to walk around to see the working mill, blacksmith shop, pioneer home, cantilever barn, corn crib, and smokehouse that have been restored in this area.

One of the most visited hikes in the Smokies - leading to the spectacular 20' falls

Trillium Gap and

Date Hiked: FALL - September 14th
Mileage: 6.4 miles Roundtrip
Our Rating: Moderate
Directions: Hwy 441 into Gatlinburg; left on Airport Road at Traffic Light #8; continue onto Cherokee Orchard Road and then onto one-way Roaring Fork Motor Nature Trail; trail is 2 miles farther on the right.

Trail Description:

The drive to this trailhead and out again on the Roaring Fork Motor Nature Trail is a delight. The beautiful, scenic road winds along the base of the mountain ridges behind Gatlinburg. There are many preserved, historic, pioneer homesteads along the route and several trails to hike on. Trillium Gap Trail is one of the access trails in the Smoky Mountains that can lead a hiker high up to Mount Le Conte and then further on to Mount Kephart and the Appalachian Trail. You may pass hikers with heavy packs coming and going on this trail. Other hikers will just be enjoying a short day hike to Grotto Falls.

The first 1.2 miles section of this trail to the falls is well traveled. It leads from the parking area up a moderate, but continual, ascent to the base of the Grotto Falls. It only gains 570 feet in elevation as it climbs, but the ascent is constant and ongoing and you may want to stop and sit on a rock for a breather on the way up. The trail is broad enough for hiking in twos or groups, and it has a firm, flat pathway, with only a few rocks and roots to navigate around, for most of the way. The early trail moves up through a deep woods with huge hardwoods and hemlocks. Roaring Fork, a swift, and steeply falling creek, runs far below to the left of the trail. There is no access to the stream until the falls but there are frequent vistas where you can enjoy watching and listening to it rush down the slopes below, churning and tossing over the rocks. You will also hear the noise of the falls as you draw near it.

Grotto Falls spews 30 feet down from a rock ledge to a pool below. It is a long, beautiful plume falls and is particularly spectacular to view when the

Grotto Falls

Smokies have had a lot of rainfall. The name of the falls comes from the rock grotto, almost like a small cave, that has developed behind and under the waterfall. The continuing trail goes directly through the grotto behind the falls, a memorable experience and a great place to take photos.

We hiked another 1.6 miles beyond the falls to Trillium Gap, the point this trail is named for. The hike is quieter here; the path narrower and steeper. You walk underneath tall, ancient hemlocks as you climb higher up Brushy Mountain and encounter stunning views at open points through the trees. In fall, the foliage dazzles with its brilliant color and in spring a profusion of wildflowers decorate the trailside. We liked this section on our hike best. We encountered fewer hikers here and enjoyed the peace and beauty of this shady woods.

Just after the 2.5 miles point, the trail crosses a small stream called Surry Fork before angling left up to Trillium Gap at 2.8 miles. A mountain gap is usually a saddle point between two ridges, and there is often a trail intersection where there is a gap. At Trillium Gap several trails fork in different directions. Trillium Gap angles on to the right, where it starts its ascent up to Mount Le Conte, and Brushy Mountain starts downward toward the Greenbrier area far below.

Before turning to start back, take the short, scenic spur trail to the left for approximately 0.4 mile. It leads out to a deadend on the top of Brushy Mountain

at approximately 4,000 feet elevation. On a clear day you will enjoy some fine vistas of nearby mountain ranges and the valley below. The return hike is all downhill and an easy one after the trek up.

Beautiful Grotto Falls

23

Porters Creek Trail

Date Hiked: FALL - September 21st
Mileage: 6 miles Roundtrip
Our Rating: Easy - Moderate
Directions: Hwy 441 to Gatlinburg; left on Hwy 321 at Traffic Light #3; right at 6 miles on Greenbrier Road; follow road 4 miles to trailhead and parking at road's end.

Trail Description:

Many of the wonderful trails off the Greenbrier Road, except possibly for the Ramsey Cascades Trail, are little known to the general public. The entire area, less frequently visited than other areas of the park, offers a wonderful place to avoid the tourist crowds and find peace and quiet on a busy day in the Smokies.

The Porters Creek Trail starts out of the back end of Greenbrier Road, passing several picnic areas along the way. The trail begins behind a gate on a wide roadbed with beautiful Porters Creek running to the left of the trail. You will hear the sounds of the stream on most of your hike and enjoy the many cascades, falls, and pools of Porters Creek along your way. We first hiked this trail in fall as the leaves were beginning to turn, but we later returned to hike it in spring when the wildflowers are a glory. The trail is famed for its many species of mountain wildflowers in the springtime. In April and early May, there are a multitude of trillium, phacaelia, phlox, dwarf iris, and showy orchis along this trail. You will also find wood betony, jack-in-the-pulpit, and rare pink and yellow lady slippers tucked off the trail sides.

This section of Greenbrier was once a settlement community called

Porters Flats and at approximately one half mile the first traces of that early community can be seen. On the right of the trail at this point stands an old rock wall, with time-worn steps that used to lead to a mountain homestead. The trail then comes to a foot-bridge creek crossing over a shallow side stream. Soon you will see another rock wall

Rare pink ladies slippers

on your right with steps through it leading to an old cemetery.

At one mile up Porters Creek, the trail comes to a broad gap and turnaround in the road. The Porters Creek Trail continues to the left along the stream. Brushy Mountain Trail angles off to the right at the back of the road loop. Also to the right of the loop turnaround is a side path leading to a preserved pioneer cabin, cantilever barn, and springhouse. The buildings are just a few yards off the trail and well-worth walking to see before continuing your hike. The historic structures are well maintained, and the grounds around the homestead are idyllic. We often stop to picnic here on the cabin's porch steps.

As Porters Creek continues after the turnaround, it begins to narrow and ascend, crossing the creek on another footbridge at 1.5 miles. This is an interesting bridge and a pretty spot. The log bridge spans high above the stream, perched on two rock boulders at either end. The trail weaves to the right and on upward through a scenic woods here. In spring, there is a sweep of white phacaelia and trillium just after the bridge crossing. After a steeper climb along the hillside, watch for Fern Falls to your left at almost 2 miles up the trail. This is a long, thin, trickley falls running 40 feet over and then down a rocky high bank. The stream from the falls crosses directly over the trail below Fern Falls. You can climb up the bank to get a closer look at the falls or just enjoy it from the trail below. If the mountains have been dry, there will be little water in the falls at all. After Fern Falls, the trail continues to climb up the ridges of Porters Mountain until it reaches Campsite #31 and the end of the trail at 3.7 miles. On our first hike up Porters Creek, we turned around a half mile after the falls at 3 miles for a 6 miles roundtrip walk.

Laurel Falls Trail

Date Hiked: FALL - September 28th
Mileage: 6.6 miles Roundtrip
Our Rating: Moderate - Strenuous
Directions: Hwy 321 to the Townsend Wye; left on Little River Road for 13.7 miles past Elkmont to the paved parking area at Fighting Creek Gap.

Trail Description:

We hiked to Laurel Falls the first time on a somewhat rainy Sunday afternoon, starting our hike in ponchos in a slight drizzle. The rain meant we could more easily find a parking place at this very popular trail, and it also meant the falls would be fuller and more spectacular from the rainfall swelling the streams.

The Laurel Falls Trail is one of the few partially paved hiking trails in the Smokies. Due to the wear and tear of continuous visitor traffic, the park had to asphalt the first 1.3 miles section of the trail leading to the falls. A hilly sidewalk now winds left and then right up the east side of Chinquapin Knob to the base of Laurel Falls. Although paved, the trail holds rough, steep sections that can be slippery in wet weather. The sharp climb surprises many novice hikers, who are pleased to discover a rest bench at just the right point along the way. From the bench, you can look off to the left of the trail to catch a view of the valley and the Little River Creek below before hiking on. Throughout the summer months and on weekends, visitors crowd the paved section of this popular trail.

The early part of the trail climbs through a shady forest and passes ancient sandstone boulders and high rocky faces along the trailside before reaching Laurel Falls at 1.3 miles. Unlike Grotto Falls, which is a long, narrow spill behind Gatlinburg, Laurel Falls is a broad, expansive waterfall, sweeping over a shelf of rock ledges to fall 75 feet. There are actually two levels of spectacular falls here, and the pathway crosses between them on a man-made bridge at the base of the main falls. The rain stopped just before we arrived, and the sun sparkled over the

26

waterfall as it came plunging down over the rocks. This is one of the most beautiful falls in the Smokies and well worth the short walk.

After the waterfall, the trail winds left along a ridge slope with views to the falls below. The trail twists as it snakes up the ridge-line away from the falls on the back-side of Cove Mountain. We walked 2 miles to Chinquapin Ridge, just past the point where the Little Greenbrier Trail intersects Laurel Falls Trail from the right at 1.8 miles. An additional walk of less than a mile takes the hiker on to the end of the trail at the park boundary where Laurel Falls Trail meets the Cove Mountain Trail at 4 miles from the original trailhead. The trail above Laurel Falls is less traveled, the path steep and narrow. Rhododendron and laurel cluster along the trailside, gradually making way for tall hardwoods. A virgin forest of huge tulip poplars, oaks, hemlocks, silverbells, and maples abound on this upper trail section.

Laurel Falls - one of the most visited sites in the Smokies

With the rain making the pathway slippery, we turned around before the trail's end, but on a less rainy day, we returned to hike to the end of the trail. Laurel Falls Trail from start to finish rises over 2,000 feet before reaching its terminus. After arriving at the final intersection at four miles, take time to turn left on Cove Mountain Trail to walk another 0.1 mile to the old fire tower, now an air monitoring station. At 4,077 feet, the 60 foot tower, built in 1935, is one of the last four remaining fire towers in the park

After hiking back to your car, you may want to drive a short distance west down Little River Road to explore the Elkmont Nature Trail on the right side of the road. Many short nature trails in the Smokies are marked with signs reading "Quiet Walkway." These delightful mini-hikes are fun, too.

Cucumber Gap Trail

Date Hiked: FALL - October 5th
Mileage: 5.8 miles Roundtrip (Loop Hike)
Our Rating: Moderate
Directions: Hwy 441 through Gatlinburg to Sugarlands Visitor Center; right on Little River Road to left into Elkmont; 1.5 miles to left at signs before campground; 0.6 mile to trailhead parking.

Trail Description:

Cucumber Gap Trail is a 2.3 miles trail that climbs up Cucumber Ridge behind Burnt Mountain to Cucumber Gap and then down again. To hike Cucumber Gap as a loop trail—often called Cucumber Gap Loop—park your car at the Little River Trail parking area where the loop route will ultimately end. Then hike 0.5 mile up the paved road past the crumbling remains of old cottages in the former Elkmont summer home community. After a steep pull to the end of the old residential road, start up the gravel trail directly behind the park gate, which is also the beginning of the Jakes Creek Trail. You will soon see the Cucumber Gap trail sign on your left at 0.3 mile beyond the gate. This walk of 0.8 mile to the Cucumber Gap trailhead is a steep one, seldom mentioned in hiking guides as part of the trail's effort or mileage. We included it in our total mileage above.

As Cucumber Gap Trail begins, it climbs up a narrow ridge path through a hardwood forest of predominantly tulip poplar trees. The yellow of the turning leaves on the October day we hiked made the forest especially pretty. After a short walk, you arrive at Tulip Branch and hop the rocks across the shal-

low creek. Watch for large wild grapevines in the trees as you continue to climb; we could imagine Tarzan loving this trail.

At 1 mile the trail arrives at its highest point, Cucumber Gap, a bridge or saddle between Burnt Mountain and Bent Arm Mountain behind Little River Valley. You will find some fine overlooks in this area across Burnt Mountain, especially in the autumn and winter after the leaves have fallen. The pathway flattens out along the ridgeline now for about a half-mile before starting a downhill march. Huge Fraser magnolia trees abound in this section with their giant, shiny, green leaves. These exotic magnolias, often nicknamed cucumber trees for their oblong, cone-shaped fruits, probably inspired the trail's name. As you walk on, the forest grows lush and deep, banked with rhododendron and ferns, the trail skittering over two small trickly streams as it descends. In the spring, wildflowers grow along the way, including wild trillium, toothwort, violets, spring-beauty, and brook lettuce. At 1.9 miles you arrive at Huskey Branch, a wider, tumbling stream, which can be crossed over a series of rocks. You may spot wild muscadine vines growing by the stream. Less than half a mile further, the trail deadends into the Little River Trail at 2.3 miles.

Across from the end of Cucumber Gap Trail is a log bench to rest on before swinging left to continue the loop hike. This part of the hike follows a broad, easy roadbed that travels gradually downhill for 1.5 miles along the Little River. You can stretch out your legs here after your climb up and over Cucumber Gap ridge.

The walk down the Little River Trail has several scenic spots along the way. Less than a half-mile from the intersection, a short bridge crosses the trail. Here Huskey Branch tumbles down the hillside in a pretty waterfall to spill into a deep green pool below in the Little River. A rustic bench sits to the left of the falls, perfectly placed to enjoy the scene. Another bench can be found farther downstream on the right of the trail, providing a fine view across the stream where cascades tumble over giant boulders. As the Little River Trail ends, you will walk down an old road through crumbling summer cottages a final time. Here you will notice park restoration efforts going on to save some of the historic homes in this area.

Rich Mountain Trail

Date Hiked: FALL - October 12th
Mileage: 6 miles Roundtrip
Our Rating: Strenuous
Directions: Hwy 321 to Townsend, right on Old Tuckaleechee Road by the Back Porch Restaurant; 1.3 miles to third right by Methodist church onto Old Cades Cove Road; follow this road up Rich Mountain to trailhead and parking area at top.

Trail Description:

This trail winds 2.3 miles up the southeast side of Rich Mountain to intersect Indian Grave Gap Trail. A half mile walk to the left on the Indian Grave Gap Trail leads to a 0.2 mile side trail that climbs to the old Rich Mountain fire tower site, a good destination point for a round trip hike of 6 miles.

A twining mountain road snakes up the northwest side of Rich Mountain to the beginning of this trail. There are many scenic views into the rural valley below and across the rolling Chilhowee and Hatcher Mountain ranges. In the fall, the colors are beautiful along this drive. At the crest of the mountain, you will find a small parking lot on the right for hikers of both Rich Mountain Trail and Ace Gap Trail.

After parking, walk 100 yards down the road to the well marked head of the Rich Mountain Trail. Behind the gate, an old roadbed swings right to start its climb up the mountainside. The trail stays broad enough for a truck or jeep to travel on all the way to the fire tower site, although the way grows rough and rocky in many places. The trail begins at 1,920 feet of elevation and ends at 3,686 feet at the tower site on the top of the mountain. You gain 1,766 feet of

elevation in the climb, most of it in the first 2.3 miles to the gap. This hike is very strenuous and all uphill with no points of relief along the journey. It is hard on the feet, ankles, and knees.

The trail switches in and out as it angles up the ridgeline. In October, the hardwood forest is ablaze with crimson, orange, and golden leaves, providing a dazzling show as you climb and offering fine panoramic views at several points. At 0.75 and 1.0 mile, look for two particularly spectacular scenes across the mountains and valley below. If the trees are not too full, you can see all the way down to Dry Valley and across to Short and Beard Cane Mountains. A narrow stream, Hesse Creek, is crossed and, depending on how wet it has been, possibly crossed again after 1.75 miles. At 2.2 miles you will arrive at the old Rich Mountain campsite, a pretty spot, with the crest of the mountain and a trail intersection just ahead.

At the intersection, the Rich Mountain Trail deadends into Indian Grave Gap Trail, which swings left to lead across the mountain and right to follow downhill to meet the one-way portion of Rich Mountain Road coming up from Cades Cove. Turn left at the intersection to hike out across the mountain. This part of the hike is the nicest, with only a gradual ascent along the ridgeline. On the left after a half-mile, you will see the side trail that leads to the old fire tower site. A short, steep climb of approximately 0.2 mile will bring you to the old fire tower site on Cerulean Knob at 3,686 feet. Only the concrete foundation of the tower remains now, and the underbrush has been allowed to grow up, obscuring the once fine views. This is disappointing, as there used to be a broad 360 degree vista here, looking in all directions out over the Smokies from this high point.

If you are not too winded from the hike up Rich Mountain, you might want to walk on further along the Indian Grave Gap Trail after visiting the tower site. But remember that the return hike back down Rich Mountain to your car is a steep downhill one and also punishing. This is no trail for beginning hikers or for anyone with health problems.

31

Baskins Creek Trail

Date Hiked: FALL - October 19th
Mileage: 6.5 miles Roundtrip (or 4 miles just to the falls and back)
Our Rating: Strenuous
Directions: Hwy 441 to Gatlinburg; left on Airport Road at Traffic Light #8; continue to Cherokee Orchard Road and then onto one-way Roaring Fork Motor Nature Trail; Baskins Creek Trail is immediately on the left as Roaring Fork Motor Nature Trail begins.

Trail Description:

The Baskins Creek Trail is another little-known and little-sung hiking trail. Easily accessible, and just behind Gatlinburg, the trail wanders through a peaceful woods and along noisy creek sides to an impressive 30 foot waterfall.

Baskins Creek Trail starts at the front end of the narrow one-way Roaring Fork Motor Nature Trail. Even when the road closes in winter, you can still get to the Baskins trailhead by walking behind the gate and up the road for 0.2 mile. From the trailhead, the single-file path winds left away from the road to climb up and over the ridge sides of Piney Mountain. It crosses Falls Branch and Baskins Creek and then swings left in a horseshoe to meet Roaring Fork Motor Nature Trail on the opposite end at 2.7 miles.

The trail begins on a single file path through a cool and quiet woods, climbing up and down in a rolling fashion for most of the first mile. The fall foliage of the maples, oaks, chestnuts, and other hardwoods are beautiful in mid October. Mixed among the hardwoods grow multitudes of pines for which Piney Mountain is named. After reaching a ridge top at 0.75 mile, the trail begins its steep, narrow, winding way down a ridge slope for a long slow mile. The slope can be slippery after heavy rains.

At one mile, the trail crosses Falls Branch. The pathway then continues steeply down the hillside, the creek running beside it. After the creek crossing, a marked trail on the left at 1.2 miles leads to an old cemetery. If you climb the steep path to see it, you will find a group of weathered stone markers on the hillside, some dating back to the early 1900s but most too obscure to read. A more

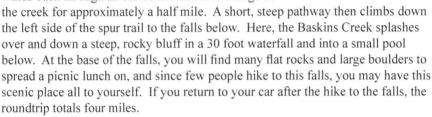

interesting and better-maintained cemetery to look for, the Bales Cemetery, lies near the end of Baskins Creek Trail approximately 50 yards from the road.

Near the halfway point on the trail, at approximately 1.3 miles, a spur trail on the left leads to the Baskins Creek Falls. This narrow trail winds back through an old homestead area alongside the creek for approximately a half mile. A short, steep pathway then climbs down the left side of the spur trail to the falls below. Here, the Baskins Creek splashes over and down a steep, rocky bluff in a 30 foot waterfall and into a small pool below. At the base of the falls, you will find many flat rocks and large boulders to spread a picnic lunch on, and since few people hike to this falls, you may have this scenic place all to yourself. If you return to your car after the hike to the falls, the roundtrip totals four miles.

For a longer 6.5 miles round trip hike, you can continue to the end of Baskins Creek Trail before turning around to start back. As you hike down Baskins Creek Trail beyond the turn to the falls, the path rolls through a shady forest for a half-mile before coming to a crossing at Baskins Creek. With no bridge, you may get your feet wet here trying to cross on the rocks when the water is high. As the trail swings right and climbs away from the creek, it passes through dense rhododendron stands. After a strenuous trek of another half mile, you finally gain the hilltop before starting a gentle descent for the last 0.4 mile to the trail's end. This last section of the trail is wider, easier, and more pleasant to hike. Remember to look for the Bales Cemetery before turning back for the return hike.

Baskins Creek Falls

33

Abrams Cooper Rd Trail

Date Hiked: FALL - November 2nd
Mileage: 7 miles Roundtrip
Our Rating: Moderate
Directions: Hwy 321 from Maryville to right on Foothills Parkway; 18 miles to end of Parkway; left on Hwy 129 for 0.2 mile to left on Happy Valley Road; turn right after 5 miles onto Abrams Creek Road and follow to Abrams Ranger Station parking area.

Trail Description:

The Cooper Road Trail is a broad pleasant hiking trail that branches out from behind the Abrams Campground, a lovely hidden away spot on the southwestern border of the national park. Many locals have never visited here before. The scenic drive to Abrams Campground crosses the full length of the Foothills Parkway over Chilhowee Mountain on the journey to the trailhead. This drive is glorious in early November with peak fall color still ablaze. There is also a lovely drive down the country road through Happy Valley below the mountain. At approximately 2.8 miles up Happy Valley Road, look for the sign for Abrams Campground on your right. Follow the narrow, snake-like road down to Abrams Creek Ranger Station where you will see several parking areas. Campers can drive back into the campground to park and camp, but day hikers cannot park in the Abrams Campground. Parking is by the ranger station, and hikers must walk 0.5 mile to the Cooper Road trailhead. The camp road, which is the first part of this hike, follows along the broad Abrams Creek and then

through the campground to a gate at the end where a park sign marks the trailhead. Inside the campground, there is a clean restroom on the left just before the trail begins.

The hike follows an old settlers' road through a deep valley between the Hatcher and Chilhowee Mountain ranges. The dirt road is nice and broad for walking, and it moves through a deep forest with a variety of hardwoods, magnolias, pines, and evergreens. In autumn, this area is a blaze of color with fall leaves crunching underfoot as you walk. In the springtime, redbuds and dogwoods are in bloom here, along with a profusion of different wildflowers. The Cooper Road Trail winds not far from the left side of Abrams Creek for the first half mile or so and then ambles along near the smaller Kingfisher Creek. Occasionally the creek or one of its small tributaries spills across the roadbed so that you need to wade the shallow water or rock hop to avoid getting your feet wet.

The roadbed trail gradually ascends. One mile from the trailhead, you will pass the intersection to the Little Bottoms Trail on the right. At 1.7 miles, the road rises to reach the Gold Mine Gap. This is an open trail intersection where the narrow Gold Mine Trail enters from the left, while the wider Cooper Road Trail continues on to the right. There are some rocks and logs to sit on here, making it a good place for a rest and lunch. Counting the initial mileage to the trailhead, you will have come 3.2 miles at this point. This is a fine place to turn around and go back for a 6.4 miles hike.

If you want to walk a little farther, continue another half mile to the next trail intersection of the Cane Creek Trail at Cane Gap, bringing your round-trip hike to 7 miles. This half mile section of the old Cooper Road drops more steeply downhill and begins to roll to the right. In spring, white arbutus and pussytoes grow along the trail here. The Cooper Road Trail is one that always seems to call you onward. A former early settlers road and Indian path, the complete trail travels 11 miles from Abrams Campground to Cades Cove Loop Road.

Gabes Mtn & Hen Wallow

Date Hiked: FALL - November 8th
Mileage: 7 miles Roundtrip (4.4 mi. to the falls and back)
Our Rating: Moderate - Strenuous
Directions: I-40E to Exit 443 at Foothills Parkway; staying on Hwy 32 to road to Cosby Campground. It is 3 miles into the campground; the trail is on the right before parking areas.

Trail Description:

After parking at the beginning of the Cosby Campground, walk back down the road about 100 yards to the Gabes Mountain sign and trailhead. The trail weaves up through Bearneck Cove between Snake Den Mountain on the left and Three Top and Round Mountain ridges on the right. The hike on Gabes Mountain Trail to Hen Wallow Falls is 2.2 miles, but we hiked on upland another 1.3 miles after visiting the falls, bringing our roundtrip mileage total to 7 miles.

Gabes Mountain Trail begins as an old, rough roadbed, narrowing as it climbs toward Gabes Mountain and Hen Wallow Falls. Some guidebooks describe this trail as relatively level with only a short climb or two, but actually the trail is a gradual and sometimes strenuous uphill walk. It first wanders through the thick woods until it comes to a fork at 0.25 mile. Stay to the right here to climb deeper in the woods before the trail falls downward to cross Rock Creek on a long log footbridge. Rock Creek is the first of many creek crossings on this trail, the early ones mostly over small tributaries of Crying Creek.

At 1 mile, you will come to a turnaround point up a short hill, just after a crossing over Crying Creek. The trail then swings back left and begins to climb more seriously to a small open area called Messer Gap, a good spot for a break before the trail begins a steep winding route along the back contours of Snake

Den Mountain. A thriving pioneer community once spread throughout this mountain area before the establishment of the park in 1934. Along the trailside, you see traces of old homesteads, rock piles, and the remains of a rock chimney. As you continue, you

36

Falls Trail

cross the final tributary of Crying Creek at approximately 1.25 miles. Be sure to look for the small falls tumbling near the crossing.

Climbing along the steep ridge from Messer Gap, you will notice rocky ledges hanging over the trailside. You may see veins of milky-white quartz in these rocks, common in some areas of the Smokies. At 2 miles on the trail, you will meet the side trail to Hen Wallow Falls. There is a trail marker on the right. Follow the spur trail along a steep slope for less than a quarter mile and then clamber down the bank to the base of the falls. A mountain stream called Lower Falling Branch plunges from a high, rocky embankment into a pool below. The creek, a mere two feet wide at the top of the falls, fans into a 20-foot wide horse-tail shape before it hits the rocks 90 feet below. The water in the pool is shallow enough for wading, and large boulders provide a convenient spot for a picnic. The amount of water tumbling over the falls varies with rainfall. Our photo was taken in a drier season.

The round trip to the falls and back is a fine 4.4 miles day hike in itself, but walking a little farther up the Gabes Mountain Trail will take you into a section of virgin forest, where you will see exceptionally larger poplars, hemlocks and silverbells, some unusually broad in diameter. The fall foliage on this section of the trail is truly spectacular and you will enjoy mossy cascades and rushing waterfalls along your way at crossings of Lower Falling Branch, Hen Wallow Creek, and Gabes Creek. We hiked 1.3 miles beyond the turn to the falls, for a 7 miles roundtrip hike including our side excursion to the falls, but on another day we hiked on to Campsite #34, a beautiful spot nestled beside a crossing of Sugar Cove Creek, 4.8 miles from the start of the Gabes Mountain trailhead. For a special ending to a hiking day in this area, bring food for a cookout in the Cosby Campground picnic area where you parked.

Hen Wallow Falls

West Prong Trail

Date Hiked: FALL - November 16th
Mileage: 5.4 miles Roundtrip (4.4 miles to Campsite 18 and back)
Our Rating: Moderate
Directions: Hwy 321 to Townsend Wye; right on Laurel Creek Road; first left at 0.2 mile onto Tremont Road; drive 2 miles to trailhead parking on right.

Trail Description:

One of the wonderful things about hiking in the Smoky Mountains are the unexpected and unplanned events that happen on your outings. On this mid November day when we hiked this trail, it started snowing while we were out on the trail and we saw our first black bear and cub lumbering through a deep valley far down below to the right of the hiking path.

West Prong Trail begins across the street from the entrance to the Tremont Institute. The 2.7 miles course rolls up and down, twining in and out around the ridgelines of Fodderstack Mountain. At first a broad lane, the trail soon narrows to a single-file path as it weaves around and hugs the ridgelines, winding through a forest of tulip poplars much of the way. The tulip-shaped leaves heavily blanketed the ground with a butterscotch yellow carpet the day we hiked. Overhead many trees still held shows of leaves in the same shade, creating a virtual wonderland of yellow fantasy as far as the eye could see. The golden leaves, dropping amid the flurries of drifting snowflakes which started as we were halfway up the trail, made this hike an unforgettable one for us.

Though not included in many hiking guides, this trail is one of our favorites, and we believe it should be celebrated more. The first mile angles right and then begins a gradual uphill ascent, hugging the left of Fodderstack

Mountain. A side path in the early part of West Prong leads approximately 100 yards to a maintained cemetery containing old gravestones dating back to the early 1800s, many with sentimental epitaphs. As you hike on

and follow the winding path up the mountain, you will enjoy sweeping views into deep dells and coves on your right. While looking down into one of these deep coves, we spotted a mother black bear and her cub walking through the woods in the valley far below and felt, admittedly, glad they were probably a half mile or more away.

At one mile, an unmaintained pathway weaves in from the right. West Prong continues straight ahead to climb over 500 feet up Fodderstack Mountain to a high point at approximately 2,000 feet. From this vantage point is a fine view into the valley below. Angling left, the West Prong then rolls down the mountain for a mile on the opposite side. Rhododendron grow along the trail here, especially near the shallow rills crossing the path at several points. One of these streams is Spicewood Branch Creek, which you rock hop in a dip between the ridges at approximately 1.5 miles.

At 2 miles, the West Prong Trail twines around a bend and into an open clearing at Campsite #18, where a wide stream rushes through a valley between two mountains. This open, scenic spot is a great place for camping, wading, or swimming. We ate our lunch here on the rocks by the water. After the campsite, the hiking trail continues by crossing over the West Prong stream on a log bridge, and you will find many picnic spots on the rocks around the bridge.

If you want to hike further, continue uphill after the campsite for 0.7 mile to the trail's end and intersection with Bote Mountain Trail. The later pathway winds steeply uphill and is rougher, rockier, and harder to hike than the previous trail section. Mountain laurel grows along this trail section, nestled under tall pines and hemlocks. The return hike retraces the same rolling ups and downs in reverse.

The Gatlinburg Trail

Date Hiked: FALL - November 23rd
Mileage: 3.6 miles Roundtrip
Our Rating: Easy
Directions: Hwy 441 to Gatlinburg bypass; at end of bypass right on 441 to first right on Park Headquarters Road just before the gray stone headquarters building and the Sugarlands Visitor Center after it; follow Park Headquarters Road all the way around to the end of the parking lot; trail begins on right from this point.

Trail Description:

This lttle-publicized walking trail proved to be a gem. The smooth, well-maintained path allows you to stretch out your legs and set a brisk walking pace. Many locals walk and jog on the Gatlinburg Trail. The broad, mostly level settlers' road follows beside the West Prong Little Pigeon River for most of its route, running through an open forest and a former homestead area. Traffic noise is surprisingly limited, even though the trail is near busy Hwy 441 and the town of Gatlinburg.

To get to the trailhead, turn onto Park Headquarters Road off Hwy 441 beside the grey stone park headquarters building. Follow the road until it dead-ends at 0.4 mile at the end of the parking lot beside a park maintenance area.

The trail begins on the right, traveling on a gravel path that soon becomes a soft footpath through a shady forest. The West Prong Little Pigeon River, running parallel to the trail, has tumbled down from the high mountains to flow through the lowlands, gaining in size and strength on its journey. At 0.3 mile on the right is a spectacular cascade where a side tributary comes plunging into the river. Stop and enjoy the stream sounds and sights at a small overlook before

continuing. Sweet-gum and sycamores line the riverbank, draping their branches gracefully over the water.

At 0.6 mile, you walk under the high overpass of the Gatlinburg Bypass Road, hardly noticing the sound of the cars above. The trail then travels alongside an old rock wall before climbing a short hill to an area that once held a small settlement of homes. Look for remains of rock steps to the left of the trail at 1 mile, followed by remnants of old chimneys and cabin foundations at 1.2 miles on the right. Stop and walk around to see the remaining foundations of the former homes that once existed along this back road. On down the trail, the path turns right to cross the river on a man-made rock bridge at 1.3 miles.

The Gatlinburg Trail next swings left to weave through the woods on the

other side of the West Prong Little Pigeon River. There are several pleasant spots along the creek banks to enjoy. You may see families picnicking or wading in the cool stream, as several side trails provide easy access to the main highway on the right. Less than a half mile from the bridge, the trail rises up gradually to a nice overlook above the creek at 1.6 miles. It then drops down again and comes out just behind River Road. Bring some money with you on this hike. You can buy an ice cream, eat lunch, or visit the tourist shops directly across the street before starting your hike back.

When you complete this short 3.6 miles hike, you can walk over and explore the one mile Fighting Creek Nature Trail.

It starts behind the Sugarlands Visitor Center at a clear trail sign to loop through the woods, over Fighting Creek on a log bridge, past a restored cabin, around a hill, and back to the Visitor Center again. It's a nice walk, particularly in the fall when the leaves are in color.

Charlies Bunion

Date Hiked: FALL - December 7th
Mileage: 8 miles Roundtrip
Our Rating: Strenuous
Directions: Hwy 441 through Gatlinburg and up the Newfound Gap Road 12+ miles to top of the mountain at Newfound Gap to the parking lot and Appalachian Trail trail sign.

Trail Description:

The hike to Charlies Bunion follows along a popular section of the Appalachian Trail, starting out of the left end of the parking lot at Newfound Gap. There are clear trail signs marking the way. If you want to encounter less hikers and tourists, and enjoy unobstructed views off the mountains, a winter day is a good time to hike this trail. However, don't plan to hike to the Bunion, as we did, on a very cold day after snow or rain. As we learned, water freezes readily in the eroded pockets between the roots and rocks along this trail, creating icy patches that make the footing hazardous and dangerous on this narrow, mountaintop trailway.

It is a strenuous 4 miles hike out to the Bunion. Many tourists begin this hike knowing very little about it and do not walk very far. The trail, which is steep and hard to hike when not in good physical shape, begins by winding northeast on the Appalachian Trail, climbing a very rocky and narrow path for the first 1.5 miles. Heavily worn from extensive hiking use, the footing is difficult. You must pick your way in and out of exposed tree roots, over and around large rocks, and carefully along extremely restricted stretches of pathway.

The trail gains 500 feet in elevation quickly by the time it reaches the first ridgetop of Mount Ambler at 1.5 miles. There is a grassy knoll here where you can take a rest. Look for

Photos on summer rehike

42

a spur trail and walk down it a short distance to see some spectacular views out over the mountains to the north. On a clear day, you can see the peaks of Mount Le Conte. The pathway drops slightly after this point and comes to an intersection with Sweet Heifer Trail, branching off to the right at 1.7 miles. This is a nice point for a rest, and there is an interesting twisted birch tree here. If you like, you can walk down Sweet Heifer Trail about a quarter of a mile to an open area with a great view down the south slopes of the mountainside toward Cherokee.

Aftert the intersection, an even steeper trail section follows up a narrow pathway over Mt. Ambler for the next mile. There are many fine views as you walk along some of the highest ridgetops in the Smoky Mountains. At 2.7 miles the Boulevard Trail swings in from the left, and at 2.9 miles, the trail arrives at a side trail on the right leading to Ice Water Spring, a fine rest point in an open area with good views. There is a camping shelter and a spring here, but you should not drink the water, as it is no longer safe. The path continues to descend past the shelter, over Masa Knob and on to the side trail out to Charlies Bunion at 4 miles.

The Charlies Bunion is an open lookout point, or rocky bald, of knobbly, jagged slate cliffs. This is your destination, and a fine place to lunch and enjoy the spectacular views to north and south of many high mountain ranges. You can see Mount Le Conte, Brushy Mountain, and the Greenbrier Pinnacle from off the Bunion. You can clamber out on the rocks here but should do so with great caution as there are 1,000 foot dropoffs and many, shaley loose stones underfoot. There have been deaths from falls off the Bunion. This trail is very popular, and the best time to hike it is on an off-season weekday. Our second hike to the Bunion, made on a summer weekday, proved more enjoyable than our first in December.

Sometimes mist enshrouds the mountains, and other times there are great views!   43

Cove Mountain Trail

Date Hiked: FALL - December 14th
Mileage: 6 miles Roundtrip
Our Rating: Moderate - Strenuous
Directions: Hwy 441 to Gatlinburg bypass; at end of bypass, right on 441 to first right on Park Headquarters Road just before the gray stone Park Headquarters building and the Sugarlands Visitor Center after it; then turn left on the first road behind the Park Headquarters building to park at trailhead just before the bridge.

Trail Description:

We discovered the beginning of this trail while looking for the Gatlinburg Trail the month before. The Cove Mountain Trail begins after crossing over the rock bridge over Fighting Creek right behind the Park Headquarters building. There is a trail sign on the right side of the road where the trailhead starts along the creekside.

It was freezing cold in the Smokies this December day, one of those days where you could see your breath in a white cloud every time you exhaled. We were bundled up in layers of clothes, including long underwear, hats, and gloves. The first quarter mile of the Cove Mountain Trail had only a gradual ascent through an open woods winding along the creek. The landscape appeared a little barren in winter, but there were evergreens, fern, and rhododendron to enjoy. Many different kinds of pine cones had fallen along the trail, and we enjoyed picking these up and trying to identify them. At only 0.2 mile we discovered Cataract Falls, a narrow 12 foot trickle of a falls sliding over a rocky

embankment in a graceful cascade. The trail twines in front of the falls, rock hops the creek, and then forks right to begin climbing the southwest ridges of Cove Mountain. After the falls, the trail narrows and becomes steeper as it climbs and curls its way up and along the ridgeline. Look for another little cascade along the route on the left where Double Gourd Branch tumbles from between the rocks.

COVE MTN TRAIL

Great Smoky Mtns

This trail is a steep climb. We warmed up quickly from the exertion even in December. There were some spectacular vistas out over Gatlinburg and up the mountain ranges to Mount Le Conte at several points. The trail opens into a wide area at about 1 mile, a good place to rest, and then turns left to climb the mountain again. You will spot park boundary markers and signs of civilization as the trail rises and you will see the backs of some mountain homes as the path follows close to a road leading to the ski resort.

The trail begins running west now up Cove Mountain and heading toward Mount Harrison. Gaining elevation with the climb, you will begin to catch several fine views out to the right and left of the trail. The forest on this section of the trail is of mixed hardwoods and pines. A variety of mosses emerge in the winter months on the forest floor and we enjoyed these as we walked. We turned around at approximately 3 miles at an opening in the woods to the right of the trail. Here there is a broad panoramic view across the Sugarlands and Bullhead Mountain

and up to the peaks of Mount Le Conte far in the distance.

Cove Mountain Trail is strenuous on the uphill climb but easier on the downhill return. We took pleasure in hiking this trail again another year in October, when the leaves were at their peak. The trail was beautiful at that season with a breathtaking show of color across the mountain ranges.

Cataract Falls

Views of Gatlinburg and Mount Le Conte

Gregory Ridge Trail

Date Hiked: FALL - December 20th
Mileage: 6 miles Roundtrip
Our Rating: Moderate - Strenuous
Directions: Take 321 into Townsend, following straight to T intersection, called the Wye, to right on Laurel Creek Road into Cades Cove Loop to Forge Creek Road just after the Visitor Center; follow 2.2 miles to the turnaround and park at the trailhead's start.

Trail Description:

In East Tennessee, no matter the season, there are many mild and pleasant days excellent for hiking. In midwinter when the trails are quieter and less trafficked, you may be the only walker on the trail, and once you begin moving the body warms up from the exertion.

It was certainly easier to get around the usually traffic-clogged Cades Cove Loop in December. We stopped to explore the old Whitehead cabin on Forge Creek Road on the left as we drove down the gravel road to park at the road's end. The Gregory Ridge Trail climbs up from the valley, at the end of the road, to rise over 2,660 feet to a gap high on top of the Smokies. To the right from the gap a trail leads 0.6 mile further to Gregory Bald, a famous destination for hikers who want to walk an 11 miles roundtrip hike.

We hiked 3 miles up Gregory Ridge Trail to a high crest with sweeping

panoramas across the valley and mountain ranges. We ate lunch at this point and then started our return for a six-mile roundtrip journey. This distance proved enough for us, since the trail requires a strenuous uphill pull most of the way. The early trail begins by winding up and around Gregory Ridge on a single file path that moves through rhododendron and laurel and then into a deep forest. The path is never far from Forge Creek on the right, although not always alongside it, and at one point at approximately 0.5 mile up the trail, Bower Creek tumbles down into Forge Creek to create a merry rush of waters and cascades. Green mosses are often at their peaks in winter when they can get light on the forest floor, so look for many varieties of these.

As the trail rises, you will begin to see some huge hardwood and evergreen trees alongside the trail as you enter a section of virgin forest. The difficult terrain spared many old trees from being timbered. At approximately 1.6 miles, the trail enters an open area and crosses Forge Creek on a long, log footbridge. The trail then swings right up a ridge above the creek to begin a series of switchbacks as it climbs the side of the mountain. There will be two more crossings of the creek in this next half mile of the trail, and the path will wind through a stand of massive tulip poplars. Some trunks are 50 inches across, and just before the third creek crossing, the trail passes right between two huge poplars.

After crossing the third log bridge, Forge Creek Campsite #12 appears on the right at approximately 2 miles. This is another nice rest point before the trail begins to climb more steeply. The next mile, and any subsequent miles you decide to hike, are strenuous as the trail now begins its final pull up the mountain to Rich Gap. Each mile gains about 800 feet in elevation.

It is worth climbing at least another mile from the campsite to enjoy some of the high vistas that open out to the right of the trailside. At approximately 2.5 miles and then again at about 3 miles, look for spectacular views out over the lower valley and mountain ranges of Hannah and Chilhowee mountains. You will find rocky boulders to rest on at these open vista spots. The return hike to the parking lot

Henry Whitehead Cabin - built in 1890s

is all steep, narrow, and downhill. This trail is a little hard for beginning hikers but beautiful at any season of the year.

47

Schoolhouse Gap Trail and

Date Hiked: WINTER - December 26th
Mileage: 7.4 mi Roundtrip (4.4 mi. roundtrip to Gap and back)
Our Rating: Moderate
Directions: Hwy 321 to Townsend Wye; right on Laurel Creek Road approximately 4 miles to parking area on right where trail-head begins.
Trail Description:

This is a popular trail and easy to find on the main road into Cades Cove. The roundtrip Schoolhouse Gap hike is a comfortable 4.4 miles hike. To add mileage and walk further, you can hike an additional 1.5 miles on an intersecting trail to a high point with fine views called Chestnut Top.

It was a sunny day with temperatures in the 50s the day we explored Schoolhouse Gap Trail the first time. The trail is a part of the mid 1800s road built to try to connect the Tennessee and North Carolina sides of the Bote Mountain. The road was never completed, but hiking trails follow its designed pathways. The trail starts on the right of the parking area along Spence Branch and winds through a valley rolling up out of Cades Cove. After a rainy spell, the first mile can be muddy and boggy. There are many mosses and ferns along this pleasant woods trail and pretty places in the stream where the water gurgles over the rocks along the way. Wildflowers

that can be found here in the springtime include white fairy wand, red cardinal flowers, Carolina vetch, and nightshade. In the late summer and fall there are wood asters, yellow ragwort, purple harebells, and sunny goldenrod.

At 1.1 miles the trail has climbed gradually to a wide place in the path called Dorsey Gap. There

Chestnut Top

was once a small settlement around this cleared area. Turkeypen Ridge Trail intersects here from the left. As Schoolhouse road continues ascending ahead, the trail becomes a little more steep and rocky underfoot. In winter when the hardwood trees are bare, there are several open vistas out to the left of the trail over to Scott Mountain.

The Schoolhouse Gap is reached at about 2 miles up the trail. The forest opens with more mountain views to the left. The Chestnut Top Trail angles off to the right of the trail at a park sign. Continue following the Schoolhouse Gap Trail on to your left. It winds around a bend to end at the park boundary line at Scott Mountain 0.2 mile later. The trail culminates behind a mountain home at the park line and a picnic table. The Scott Mountain Trail begins just beyond in the woods ahead, swinging left up the ridge line to continue on out over Scott Mountain.

On the return hike, if you are not tired, swing left on Chestnut Top Trail at the gap and walk out another 1.5 miles or more on this nice trail. It is a delightful, pine-needle strewn pathway that winds along the mountain top to Bryant Gap and then on to Chestnut Top at 1.5 miles. The trail is almost flat, curling enticingly through a beautiful pine woods. It winds up along the park boundary on the ridgetop with views of the southern mountain ranges and Tuckaleechee Cove and valleys to the left. Even more panoramic views can be seen on the right side of the trail of Smokies peaks like Fodderstack, Bote, and Thunderhead mountains. In winter when the foliage is sparse, the views are even more spectacular. It is a quiet and beautiful trail not to miss.

Old Sugarlands Trail

Date Hiked: WINTER - December 28th
Mileage: 6 miles Roundtrip
Our Rating: Moderate - Strenuous
Directions: Hwy 441 to Gatlinburg bypass; at end of bypass right on 441 to first right on Park Headquarters Road just before the gray stone headquarters building and the Sugarlands Visitor Center; park by headquarters building; walk back out to Hwy 441 and across the road; turn back toward Gatlinburg and walk a short distance to trail sign on right of the road.

Trail Description:

Very few hiking books mention the Old Sugarlands Trail in their trail descriptions. This is a shame because the trail is easy to get to and is an interesting hike.

A short walk toward Gatlinburg from the park headquarters building on Hwy 441 near Gatlinburg leads to the beginning of the Old Sugarlands Trail on the right. The early part of the trail is scenic and varied, passing rock cliffs and following a woods trail along the West Prong Little Pigeon River. You will enjoy this flat streamside walk. In the first quarter mile, watch for a split in the trail and stay right on the lower trail to remain on Old Sugarlands. As you follow the stream, you will see high rock bluffs, once a part of an old quarry, rising over 70 feet high to the left of the path. Just before the half mile mark, the trail swings left and away from the stream and rises up a hill to a trail intersection. At the intersection, make an abrupt right down a short, steep embankment to continue following Old Sugarlands Trail. After scrambling down the bank, the pathway curls back toward the stream again to begin its journey through an

old pioneer settlement area. As we hiked into the settlement area, snow began to fall.

Old Sugarlands Trail winds through open woods and scenic fields in this section, and the path gradually widens into an old dirt road as it reaches back toward the settlement. The path rock-crosses Thirst Branch Creek at

0.8 mile, curling through hardwoods and past many sugar maple trees that the trail is named for. At 1 mile, Bullhead Branch flows under a trail culvert. The woodland is open and appealing here, and you can easily imagine the cabins and farms that once populated this area. In the springtime, an abundance of wildflowers flourish along the trail.

At 1.5 miles, Old Sugarlands broadens and becomes a macadam roadbed. The ongoing Old Sugarlands Trail turns left up this paved road. A spur trail leads on ahead along the West Prong Little Pigeon River and back to a historic area where the Pi Beta Phi Settlement School, built from the Brackins log school, the Sugarlands Cemetery, and other settlement buildings used to be. We later explored this area on a sunny spring day, finding the old clock tower, remnants of several structures, and the rock house off an unmarked side trail.

By now, our December snowfall was thickening and beginning to totally cover the ground. As we started up the paved road, we could still see the old walls, bridge foundations, and other evidences of the Sugarlands settlement and the two CCC camps that once operated in this area. This section of the trail is quite steep. The road climbs continually and somewhat relentlessly, gaining 500 feet in the first mile. We had planned to hike to the trail's end at 3.9 miles before turning around, but because the snow was getting deep so quickly, we turned down the Two-Mile Branch Trail at 3.3 miles, hoping to cut back quickly to Hwy 441 and our car. This 2.6 miles detour route followed Two Mile Branch on a downhill journey to bring us out on the highway. We had to also walk another half mile out from the horse stable and then on up the road, so we didn't save much time with our shortcut. The downhill trail we chose was rutted out and rough with gullies hidden under the snow. It was a long cold way back, snowing the entire time.

Our second hike on Sugarlands in the spring was much more enjoyable. We hiked the 3.9 miles trail to its end at Cherokee Orchard Road and also walked the side path to the settlement area and rock house.

Ace Gap Trail

Date Hiked: WINTER - January 3rd
Mileage: 6 miles Roundtrip
Our Rating: Easy to Moderate
Directions: Hwy 321 from Maryville to Townsend; right on Old Tuckaleechee Road at Back Porch Restaurant; 1.3 miles to third right by Methodist church onto Old Cades Cove Road; follow this road up Rich Mountain to trail and parking area at dead end at top.

Trail Description:

Winding around the ridgeline of Rich Mountain and working its way over to Kelly Gap campsite and on across Rich Mountain, Ace Gap Trail begins directly out of the back of the parking area at a trail sign. The narrow single-file trail is mostly easy to walk. Thick with leaves or pine needles underfoot in winter, the path rises in a steady ascent for the first mile, sometimes a little steeply, before leveling out to rise and fall in an undulating fashion for the next mile and a half. Several dips go down to cross small streams over the rocks, then up again in roller-coaster fashion.

There are few points to clock mileage along this trail, which curves left and then loops back right as it journeys toward Kelly Ridge. Just before reaching Kelly Gap watch for a huge pine tree, 30 inches in diameter. The trail drops gradually before growing quite steep as it nears the gap. Since most of the trail

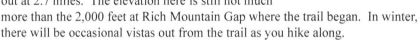

previously has been somewhat flat or gently rolling, you will notice this change and realize you are nearing the gap. Kelly Gap and Campsite #4 are at 2.2 miles down in a dell. It's a nice spot to rest for lunch. After the campsite, the trail begins to climb up and out of the gap and over the next ridge. The trail flattens out at 2.7 miles. The elevation here is still not much more than the 2,000 feet at Rich Mountain Gap where the trail began. In winter, there will be occasional vistas out from the trail as you hike along.

We turned around on this first hike at 3 miles up Ace Gap Trail where the path nears a boundary road coming from the valley below. Another day we continued on for a longer hike to Ace Gap, the spot the trail is named for. The trail stays relatively the same in elevation for the next mile but snakes in and out around the ridgelines. It then drops abruptly to Ace Gap at 4.7 miles. In the gap is Campsite #7 where loggers once played cards far from the eyes of the disapproving townsfolk, giving this trail its name. A shallow stream lies behind the campsite and you may see evidence of the old railroad that once rose to the gap. This is a good trail choice for novice hikers.

Ace Gap, 5.6 miles in length, is pretty to hike in any season. In winter, there are fine views, in April and May beautiful wildflowers including rare pink ladies slippers, in summer deep shade on a hot day, and in fall spectacular color foliage.

Meigs Mountain Trail

Date Hiked: WINTER - January 11th
Mileage: 6 miles Roundtrip
Our Rating: Moderate
Directions: Hwy 441 through Gatlinburg to Sugarland Visitor Center; right on Little River Road to left at Elkmont sign; 1.5 miles to trail signs just before campground entrance and turn left at signs; drive 1 mile to end of road and parking area for trailhead.

Trail Description:

Less known than other trails in the Elkmont area, this trail rolls through a low area between Meigs Mountain to the south and the Curry He and Curry She Mountains to the north. Meigs Mountain Trail follows the Oconaluftee fault and many homesites used to be scattered along this valley. Meigs Mountain Trail is an enjoyable and easy hike, gaining only moderate elevation as it rolls gently up and down through the forest from Elkmont to Buckhorn Gap, where it intersects with the end of Meigs Creek Trail at 8.7 miles.

To reach the beginning of the trail, you begin by hiking strenuously uphill 0.5 mile on the early roadbed section of Jakes Creek Trail. After passing the intersection of Cucumber Gap Trail on the left, watch for a clear trail sign for Meigs Mountain Trail on the right. Here the pathway drops steeply downhill and then winds around through the woods to cross tumbling Jakes Creek on a rustic footbridge at 0.3 mile past the trailhead. The stream is tree-lined and shady with rhododendron all along the banks. A secondary trail here leads off to the right just after the bridge to a park service area and another less recommended route into the trail area.

Continuing left on Meigs Mountain Trail, the path begins to ascend up the back ridges of Meigs Mountain, rising in an undulating pattern so that it

never becomes too strenuous. The hike passes through many cleared spots with stone founda-tions and fences of old homesites. It often follows, and then rockhops, several creeks along the way. Look for a small cascades in the

first half mile. The hardwood forest is beautiful with rich varieties of fern and mosses. In spring, you will see wildflowers as well as sweeps of daffodils. Each part of the trail has its own character. You pass through sections rich with hemlocks and evergreens and then move through areas shaded by poplar and oaks. In some spots, you walk through lush rhododendron groves or beside hillsides covered in laurel. Little coves and hollows drop off attractively to either side of the trail.

After the first mile, the trail winds up and around a rocky ridge thick with rhododendron and down to King Branch Campsite #20 at 1.6 miles. At the campsite, Blanket Creek and Kiver Branch meet in a tumble. Look for fruit trees here that settlers once planted, and watch for sourwood trees

Deer grazing at Elkmont Campground.

as you climb the next half mile out of the campsite. In winter, there are views here out to the left of Meigs Mountain. At 2.5 miles, the trail levels out again.

Rain began to mist at this point, so we turned around before the trail met the Curry Mountain Trail at 3.2 miles. Our return was in a light rain all the way— a wise reason to always pack rain ponchos!

Finley Cane Trail

Date Hiked: WINTER - January 25th
Mileage: 5.6 miles Roundtrip
Our Rating: Moderate
Directions: Hwy 321 to Townsend Wye; right on Laurel Creek Road approximately 6 miles to where trailhead begins; there are pull-over parking spaces on the roadsides.

Trail Description:

Three trails begin at this same area off Laurel Creek Road. Finley Cane, on the left, rises up from Big Spring Cove to angle left and climb the west slope of Bote Mountain. At 2.8 miles, it meets the Bote Mountain Trail.

Best hiked after a week or two of dry weather in the Smokies, Finley Cane Trail can be very muddy—and not just in a few spots—if there has been heavy rain or snow in the mountains. Its use as a horse trail further mucks up the path in wet weather. The day we hiked we had to skirt around many muddy areas in the trail, spoiling some of the enjoyment of this nice hiking trail.

The trail has gradual climbs, flat stretches, and little downhill climbs to five creek crossings: Sugar Cove Prong, Sugar Cove Branch, Laurel Cove Creek, Hickory Tree Branch, and Finley Cove Creek. Some are wider and more rushing than others, and all but one must be rock-hopped. This can be a little tricky when the creeks are high, but with care, you can avoid wet feet. The trail rises and falls through evergreens, rhododendron groves, mixed open forest and deep

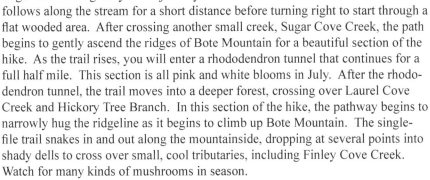

woods with many mature, towering hemlocks, pines, oaks, and tulip trees. There are scenic coves rolling down from the ridgeline path and pretty vistas out over Rich and Scott Mountains at several points along the way.

At first Finley Cane winds through the woods almost parallel to the road, crossing shallow Sugar Cove Prong early on its journey. The trail then follows along the stream for a short distance before turning right to start through a flat wooded area. After crossing another small creek, Sugar Cove Creek, the path begins to gently ascend the ridges of Bote Mountain for a beautiful section of the hike. As the trail rises, you will enter a rhododendron tunnel that continues for a full half mile. This section is all pink and white blooms in July. After the rhododendron tunnel, the trail moves into a deeper forest, crossing over Laurel Cove Creek and Hickory Tree Branch. In this section of the hike, the pathway begins to narrowly hug the ridgeline as it begins to climb up Bote Mountain. The single-file trail snakes in and out along the mountainside, dropping at several points into shady dells to cross over small, cool tributaries, including Finley Cove Creek. Watch for many kinds of mushrooms in season.

The upper trail has the best views, and at 2 miles the footpath passes by big grapevines and bamboo-like cane stands the trail is named for. At this point, you will begin to see some large hemlocks and oaks along the trail, plus many tulip poplars as large as two feet in diameter. The foliage on this section of the trail is beautiful in the fall. In the last half mile is a ridgetop clearing, with piles of flat rocks, that makes a terrific picnic site and rest stop. A short distance farther, at 2.8 miles, the trail ends, running into the lower end of the Bote Mountain Trail. The mostly downhill return is easier than the hike in.

We have hiked Finley Cane in many seasons, and it is now one of our favorite trails in the Smokies. In every season there is something special to discover and enjoy.

57

Cades Cooper Road Trail

Date Hiked: WINTER - February 1st
Mileage: 5.4 miles Roundtrip (6 miles with the side trip to the Oliver Cabin)
Our Rating: Moderate
Directions: Hwy 321 to Townsend Wye; right on Laurel Creek Road and onto Cades Cove Loop; trailhead is 4.3 miles on right with pullover parking.

Trail Description:

The 11 miles long Cooper Road Trail is an old roadbed that once acted as a main access for settlers from the cove to Happy Valley and on to Maryville across the Chilhowee Mountain. We had hiked the Abrams end of the Cooper Road (Abrams Cooper Road Trail) and enjoyed it, so on this February day we found the Cades Cove end of the same trail and hiked it to Stony Ridge. It was a good choice for a weekend walk following heavy snows and melt-off in the Smokies, when many other dirt pathways would have been too wet and muddy for pleasurable hiking.

Cooper is a smooth, open road trail on which you can stretch out your stride and walk easily two-by-two or in a group. It weaves gradually uphill through pines, maples, oaks, and poplars. We saw huge holly trees and many other hardwoods and evergreens. In winter, the forest is a little barren, but in fall the trees are a blaze of color and in spring there are wildflowers along the trail.

The trail winds up and down, crossing four streams and small creeks, one just drizzling over the roadbed. The path angles left in the first mile as it starts its journey northwest. On the left at approximately 0.2 mile watch for a nice one mile side trail, Wet Bottom Trail, that leads to the historic Elijah Oliver cabin in 0.3 mile and then over to the Abrams Falls Trail in another half mile. At the old homestead, built by Elijah Oliver in 1866, you can walk around to see the well-preserved cabin, barn, springhouse, and smokehouse.

After the Wet Bottom intersection, the trail continues left and then switches right, crossing Kingfisher Creek along the way. As you work your way around and over the ruts and rocky spots in the trail, imagine what it would be like to travel in a wagon over this roadbed trail. At approximately 1 mile the trail switches left again after dipping down to cross Arbutus Branch. The path then rises, jig-jagging left and switching back sharply right as it rises to Arbutus Ridge. Having gradually attained almost 1,000 feet in elevation since the start, you may begin to catch some views off the trail here, or further on, when you attain the top of Stony Ridge at approximately 2.6 to 2.7 miles. For a longer hike, you can continue uphill another 3 miles to the junction of Hannah Mountain Trail on the left and Beard Cane Trail on the right. We turned around for our return at Stony Ridge, after lunching on a big log there.

Spruce Flats Falls

Date Hiked: WINTER - February 22nd
Mileage: 4 miles Roundtrip (3 miles just to the falls and back)
Our Rating: Strenuous - but worth it!
Directions: Hwy 321 to Townsend Wye; right on Laurel Creek Road; first left at 0.2 mile onto Tremont Road; 2 miles to left to parking at Tremont Institute.

Trail Description:

This short trail is not written up in any of our hiking guides. We learned of the falls in a happenchance conversation and then went looking for the trailhead. From the parking area, walk right ap-proximately 0.2 mile down the road until it almost ends. Watch for a sign on the left leading up into the woods that simply reads: Falls Trail. Follow the trail from here as it winds behind Tremont Institute, past the water tank, and up a ridge behind Meigs Mountain. Stay on the main path and avoid side paths for the first half-mile. The trail climbs gradually uphill behind the institute and then begins a strenuous march over a steep ridge. There is occasional moderation from straight climbing but not much. The trail is single file and often narrow,

with large rocks and tree roots to struggle over along the way.

As Spruce Flats Falls Trail climbs the ridge, it crosses two rocky rills and passes several fine overlooks. Pausing at these open points on the trail, you can see over the mountain ranges to Thunderhead Mountain and down into the valley to the

Middle Prong Little River and Tremont Road. At approximately 2 miles, the top of the ridge is reached at a tree trunk decorated with name carvings. These are probably the names of Girl Scouts who attended Camp Margaret Townsend through the 1950s in what is now Tremont Institute. After crossing the ridgetop, you begin a sharp descent to Spruce Flats Falls, which you will hear before you see. Four mountain streams, Spruce Flats Branch, Honey Cove Branch, Turner Branch, and Deep Camp Branch, have tumbled down from higher elevations of the Smokies to merge and surge into a series of cascading waterfalls dropping over a rocky face into the Middle Prong. Four different cascades form Spruce Flats Falls. The first and tallest, a plunge waterfall, spreads 60 feet wide and drops 60 feet in height to splash into a broad, deep pool at the base of the falls. Beyond the first waterfall and pool, three more cascade levels follow as the water riots downhill over rocky ledges and boulders.

The waterfalls are some of the most beautiful in the Smokies. Large rocks and boulders all around the falls' base and stream provide vantage points on which to sit and enjoy the spectacular water show while having a backpack lunch. A trail continues on the other side of the stream. No markers indicated where it went or how far it traveled. We walked it another 0.5 mile as it wound high along Wilkerson Ridge and then returned back to the falls for the return hike. After returning, check out the GSMA Tremont Store for books, apparel, and gift items.

Spruce Flats Falls

Rich Mountain Loop by

Date Hiked: WINTER - February 15th
Mileage: 6.8 miles Roundtrip (3 mi. roundtrip to the Oliver Cabin)
Our Rating: Moderate
Directions: Hwy 321 to Townsend Wye; right on Laurel Creek Road; 7.5 miles to start of Cades Cove Loop; trailhead is on right after end of parking lot.

Trail Description:

      Park as close to the start of the Cades Cove Loop Road as possible to begin this section of the Rich Mountain Loop Trail. The trailhead starts at a

signpost at the edge of the parking area on the right. We first hiked this trail in mid February after a heavy snow had blanketed the mountains. Our going was slow because of the snow-covered, sloppy, and muddy sections along the trail. Rich Loop is a lovely trail; we returned to hike it again in spring and it was much nicer. In fine weather, hikers can stretch out their stride on the first, almost flat, miles of the trail. There are four stream crossings to rock-hop or wade, and some are rather wide. High water may increase the difficulty of the crossings.

      A short distance after passing the initial trail sign, the pathway angles

left to travel east along the border of the woods. You can see cleared pasture areas on the left through the trees. At a quarter mile look carefully for a huge mound across the fields, often called "the Indian mound" though never proven to be a Cherokee burial site. After the mound, the trail curls

Oliver Cabin

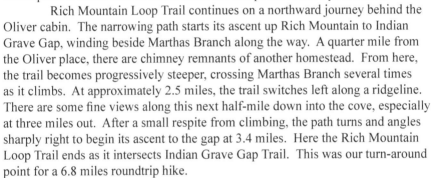

right through an open woods to cross Crooked Arm Branch and intersect with the Crooked Arm Ridge Trail on the right at 0.5 mile. The Loop Trail turns left again here, crosses Harrison Branch and later re-crosses it before the trail opens out into a clearing to arrive at the John Oliver cabin at 1.5 miles. The historic cabin, preserved by the park, was built in the early 1800s. You can explore it inside and sit on the front or back porch to have your lunch.

Rich Mountain Loop Trail continues on a northward journey behind the Oliver cabin. The narrowing path starts its ascent up Rich Mountain to Indian Grave Gap, winding beside Marthas Branch along the way. A quarter mile from the Oliver place, there are chimney remnants of another homestead. From here, the trail becomes progressively steeper, crossing Marthas Branch several times as it climbs. At approximately 2.5 miles, the trail switches left along a ridgeline. There are some fine views along this next half-mile down into the cove, especially at three miles out. After a small respite from climbing, the path turns and angles sharply right to begin its ascent to the gap at 3.4 miles. Here the Rich Mountain Loop Trail ends as it intersects Indian Grave Gap Trail. This was our turn-around point for a 6.8 miles roundtrip hike.

For a longer 8.5-miles roundtrip and to complete the loop hike, turn right and hike 2.5 miles on Indian Grave Gap Trail to the Crooked Arm Ridge Trail intersection. Turn right on Crooked Arm to hike 2.1 miles back down the steep ridge to intersect Rich Mountain Loop again. Then turn left to walk the final 0.5 mile back to the trailhead and your car. The full loop hike is challenging unless you are in good physical shape and hike often.

Historic John Oliver Cabin

Roundtop Trail

Date Hiked: WINTER - February 28th
Mileage: 5 miles Roundtrip
Our Rating: Moderate
Directions: Hwy 321 to Townsend Wye; left on Little River Road to Metcalf Bottoms picnic area on left; turn in to picnic area and continue straight, crossing bridge and following road that becomes Wear Cove Road for 1 mile to the trail sign; park on roadside.

Trail Description:

It's easy to miss the Roundtop Trail sign on the climb up Wear Cove Road, and there is no designated parking lot. You can park on the roadside before the trail or just up the hill from the trailhead at the Little Greenbrier pullover. Roundtop, a little-known and little-hiked trail, is one of our favorites, and we have hiked it several times in different seasons. Winter, when we first hiked Roundtop, is a good time to do the trail because the leaves are down and the views are better. The easily walked scenic forest trail weaves its way up and around the ridgelines on Roundtop Mountain, which is the mountain range between the Wear Cove valley on the north and the Little River valley on the south. Picturesque views along the trail often look off into these valleys and on to the mountain ranges beyond them.

The single-file path is mostly an uphill climb, but there are occasional flatter stretches for relief as the trail works its way to 2,500+ feet in elevation to

Joint Ridge at 2.5 miles. The trail winds south-east through pines, oaks, dogwoods, laurel, and across two drizzly creek branches. We enjoyed the diverse varieties of mosses, plants, and pines, plus the birdsongs along this trail. We even saw a grouse.

The first half-mile rises steadily from the road up the eastern flank of Roundtop Mountain, but then the hike moderates, rolling in and around the ridge sides in S's. You will catch glimpses out to Cove Mountain and up to Roundtop Mountain's crest as you climb. At 0.5 mile, Roundtop Trail reaches the park boundary, with markers along the trailside. The single-file pathway ascends soon afterwards to an open knob right behind a vacation home. Stop to look at the views down into Wears Valley from here.

Past the house, the trail angles left and starts uphill again, continuing to wind in and out of the forest along the steep ridge sides until it turns right to arrive at Joint Ridge, an open cliff with large boulders at 2.5 miles. Panoramic views abound before the trail curls farther right along the ridgeline. This ridge is a good point for lunch and a fine place to turn around for a 5 miles day hike. For a longer walk, continue a mile or two as the trail curls around and then begins descending the ridgetop. Be watchful on this trail section as the way grows very narrow in spots, especially at 3.5 miles. Eventually at 7.5 miles, Roundtop drops sharply to end at the Townsend Wye where the river is too deep and swift to cross on foot.

Little Greenbrier Trail

Date Hiked: SPRING - March 22nd
Mileage: 6 miles Roundtrip
Our Rating: Moderate - Strenuous
Directions: Hwy 321 to Townsend Wye; left on Little River Road to Metcalf Bottoms picnic area on left; turn in to picnic area and continue straight, crossing bridge and following to top at Wear Cove Road; park on right pullover at trailhead.

Trail Description:

Little Greenbrier is another seldom-hiked and little-known trail. The 4.3 miles journey from Wear Cove Road to the intersection of Laurel Falls Trail is an uphill trek all the way. We hiked 3 miles of the trail before turning to start back to our vehicle.

The single-file path of Little Greenbrier Trail begins by winding gradually along the ridgelines of Little Mountain. Pines and evergreens shaded the way and we enjoyed stopping to look at stretches of rich moss along the trailside. Signaling the arrival of spring, the hardwood trees sported new green leaves and buds. By mid April, the leaves will be fully out with wildflowers along the trailside. However, a hike in March offers better views. To the left you can see glimpses of Wears Valley and the mountains through the still bare trees. You will also note park boundary signs along this early section of the walk, as Little Greenbrier Trail follows close along park boundary lines.

At 1.9 miles the narrow pathway opens into a broad intersection where trails converge from all directions. Little Brier Gap Trail comes up from

Metcalf Bottoms to end here, and a side trail we've heard locals call Buckeye Springs drops off north, heading toward Wears Valley and Bridgemont Camp. The Little Greenbrier Trail continues to the east, angling right and straight up the hill. At this intersection, several fallen logs and large rocks offer a nice resting spot or a place to eat lunch.

The continuing Little Greenbrier Trail is steep and strenuous from this point on. It attains an elevation of approximately 1,330 feet as it travels southeast, zig-zagging around the ridgelines in several swithchbacks along the way. This 2.4 miles section follows a narrow, single-file, dirt path, rutted and rocky, and not easy to walk. As the tight path rises up Chinquapin Ridge on Cove Mountain, you will encounter several open points where you can look out to the north across the mountains and see panoramic views down into Wears Valley and over to Cove Mountain. In the fall the rich gold and red of the foliage is outstanding on this upper section of the trail.

As the march uphill nears the 3 miles point, you may notice interesting outcroppings of rock called Metcalf Phyllite, metamorphosed shale. Past this rocky section the trail opens out and you will find another fine vista out over the mountains and valley below. We stopped here to lunch and rest before starting our walk back. Although the return is all downhill, steep downhill climbs are often as strenuous as steep uphill ones, making this a somewhat difficult hike for those not in good physical shape.

Good spot for a lunch break at Little Brier Gap

Grapeyard Ridge Trail

Date Hiked: SPRING - March 29th

Mileage: 6.4 miles Roundtrip

Our Rating: Moderate

Directions: Hwy 441 to Gatlinburg; left on Hwy 321 at Traffic Light #3; right at 6 miles on Greenbrier Road; drive 3.2 miles to trailhead just across from bridge to Ramsey Cascades Trail; small pullover parking on the left of road.

Trail Description:

The Grapeyard Ridge Trail winds westward for 7.5 miles to eventually connect to the Roaring Fork Nature Trail behind Gatlinburg. A nice day hike is to go 3.2 miles to Injun Creek Campsite #32 and back. We first hiked Grapeyard Ridge on a warm day in early spring with temperatures in the 70s and blue skies overhead.

The first half mile is a little strenuous, climbing up away from the road, into the woods, and up a ridge. Along the trail you will see traces of the settlers who once lived in this area: rock walls, foundations, and even rusting artifacts. After 0.5 mile the trail moderates, descending the same ridge and crossing early

tributaries of Rhododendron Creek at 0.8 mile and at 0.9 mile over the rocks. The trail then rolls into a broad valley along Rhododendron Creek and its tributaries. Many mountain families once lived along this green valley between Blazed Pine and James Ridge on the north and Potato Ridge and Brushy Mountain on the south. You may see traces of the rock walls and cleared fields where their houses and barns once lay, just as you saw traces of settlement life earlier on the trail. It is easy to see why early pioneers chose this place. The stream gurgles and sings alongside the trail, and wildflowers riot all over the meadows. Spring beauties covered the ground when we hiked in late March and white starry-shaped bloodroot clustered in abundance by the creeks. Yellow buttercups spread in sweeps among mayapples, pussy toes, and trillium nearly ready to bloom. Marsh blue violets and yellow violets grew in colorful clumps along the trail, big trees overhung the creek banks along this green bottomland, and the mountains rose up behind the valley like great, misty protectors, making this a pleasant place to sit and dream.

At about 1 mile, the trail begins to gently ascend out of the valley, passing through rhododendron and crossing over Rhododendron Creek. As the path rises through thicker forest, it follows along the creek, crisscrossing it several more

times. The trail begins rising more steeply at 2 miles to climb up to reach James Ridge and then James Gap at 2.7 miles. It then drops downward to make the first crossing of Injun Creek. You may see scattered remnants of what was once an old steam engine in and around the creek. Grapeyard Ridge Trail now winds its way down the side of James Ridge, skittering in and out of the woods and over little tributaries of Injun Creek. Sometimes these tributaries and the trail seem to run together, and in rainy seasons this trail section may be muddy. When the trail begins to level out, you will know you are nearly to Campsite #32, which is off a short side trail to the right in a wide, open area beside the rushing water of Injun Creek. You can sit on the bank or

on a big rock in the creek to enjoy lunch before beginning the hike back.

69

Chestnut Top Trail

Date Hiked: SPRING - April 12th
Mileage: 5.6 miles Roundtrip
Our Rating: Strenuous - Moderate
Directions: Hwy 321 to the parking area on left just before the Townsend Wye intersection; the trailhead is on the right across the street from parking lot.

Trail Description:

Finding a place to park is sometimes a problem for Chestnut Top Trail, which begins across from the Townsend Wye parking lot, since the Wye draws crowds of tubers and swimmers. You can see the trail extending directly up a steep ridge from the highway. Hikers should watch their footing carefully as they climb. The first 0.5 mile angles sharply uphill on a narrow pathway before arriving at an abrupt switchback and then levels out for the next 0.5 mile. The trail then begins to ascend, first gradually and then steeply as it rises to crest Chestnut Top.

The beginning of the trail, although steep and strenuous, draws many hikers because of the abundance of wildflowers seen along the cliffs. Park rangers say 40 species or more grow on the first mile alone. April is the best time to see the wildflowers. On the mid April day we first hiked the trail, we saw purple dwarf iris, trillium, phacelia, white and yellow violets, wood betony with its

ferny leaves, hepatica, fire pinks (which are actually red), Solomon's seal that look like white bells, pussy toes, delicate bishop's-cap, stonecroft with its succulent leaves, toothwort, and many other wildflower varieties. Using our wildflower guidebook as we walked up the hillside, we also identified squaw root, chickweed, spring beauty, bloodroot, and even little brown jug hidden in the leaves among white anemone.

After the switchback at 0.5 mile, the trail travels southeasterly through an open forest above the highway and then winds right to start climbing up the ridgeline of Scott Mountain. This section of the trail is very pretty with pines, hardwoods, mosses, interesting plants, flowers, and thick rhododendron. As the trail winds higher up a pine-strewn and soft-footed path, picture-window views open out over the mountains and Cades Cove. At 1.5 miles the trail becomes much steeper. It weaves in and out around the ridgeline, making the climb more enjoyable as it rises to an elevation of 2,500 feet at Chestnut Top at 2.8 miles. This ridgetop knoll is a good spot to break your hike. The downhill return is pleasant and easy, creating a comfortable 5.6 miles roundtrip hike. For a longer walk, you can continue across the ridgelines to the end of the trail at 4.3 miles where it intersects Schoolhouse Gap Trail, creating a roundtrip journey of 8.6 miles.

This is a popular springtime hike for wild flowers

Turkeypen Ridge Trail

Date Hiked: SPRING - May 31st
Mileage: 7.2 miles Roundtrip
Our Rating: Easy - Moderate
Directions: Hwy 321 to Townsend Wye; right on Laurel Creek Road about 5.5 miles; the trail sign and parking pullover is on the right.
Trail Description:

After over a month of rains and time off the trails, we returned to our weekend hikes, choosing a non-strenuous trail in the Cades Cove area for our first time back out. Turkeypen Ridge Trail travels southwesterly toward Townsend, angling to the right off Laurel Creek Road and dead-ending into Schoolhouse Gap Trail at 3.6 miles.

The trail travels from the parking area on a level woods path that soon climbs gradually in and out around the bases of Pinkroot Ridge and, later, Turkeypen Ridge. The trail was once called Pinkroot Trail after the first ridge base it follows and for the pinkroot herbaceous flowers that like the moist soils here in the mountains. Cherokees and settlers often used the pink roots of these red tubular flowers, also called Indian pinks, for medicinal purposes.

In the first 0.5 mile, the path winds from Big Spring Cove through a rich, green woods—very green in May—and crosses Crib Gap Trail and two stream branches that lead down to Laurel Creek. Then the trail climbs up and around Pinkroot Ridge to drop down to a crossing of Pinkroot Branch just before reaching 1.5 miles. The hardwood and pine woods are more open here with

72

several grassy field areas and some rest logs and rock ledges nearby for a hiking break.

Numerous wildflowers grow along the trail side: white vetch, milky galax spires with their big heart-shaped evergreen leaves, patches of bluets, yellow hawkweed, and daisy-like clusters of wood asters. Watch for squawroot, an odd parasitic plant that grows near the base of trees and looks like yellow ears of corn. In season, you may also see rhododendron, mountain laurel, or flame azaleas in bloom.

None of the creek crossings are broad on this path; most are less than an-kle-deep and easily crossed. After the Pinkroot Branch crossing, the path wanders through a gradually ascending area before beginning to rise steeply up Turkeypen Ridge. At the top of the ridge, at approximately 3 miles, is an open area with nice rest logs for lunch. The last piece of the trail drops downhill to meet Schoolhouse Gap Trail at Dorsey Gap, your turnaround point for this hike. Turkeypen Ridge Trail is diverse all along the way, first broad and then narrow, soft underfoot in some areas while rocky and rough in others. This gently undulating trail is a delight at any season.

Rare Jack-in-the-Pulpit
One of many rare flowers
sometimes found on the side
of hiking trails - keep your
eyes open!

Rabbit Creek & Hannah

Date Hiked: SUMMER - June 7th
Mileage: 8.6 miles Roundtrip
Our Rating: Strenuous
Directions: Hwy 321 from Maryville to right on Foothills Parkway; 18 miles to end of Parkway; left on Hwy 129 for 0.2 mile to left into Happy Valley; turn right after 5 miles onto Abrams Creek Road and follow to Abrams ranger station parking area.
Trail Description:

Exploring the hiking trails in the Smokies often brings unexpected adventures. One of the reasons we decided to write this book is so hikers might avoid problems like we encountered on this trip when we came to a deep, wide, turbulent stream too dangerous to cross. Based on our trail research, we had planned to do a loop hike up Rabbit Creek, left on Hannah Mountain, across Abrams Creek, down Little Bottoms Trail, and left on Cooper through Abrams Campground and back to our car. Instead we turned around at the Abrams Creek crossing when we found the stream impassable. However, despite surprises along the way, we enjoyed this hike in the Abrams Creek area of the Smokies.

The Rabbit Creek Trail, which begins immediately across from the ranger station, travels a journey of 7.6 miles from Abrams Campground over Pine Mountain and Coon Butt to drop down into the back of Cades Cove. The path at first

Mountain Trails

wanders down an old settlers' road for a short distance before crossing a wide, deep span of Abrams Creek on a long footbridge, as the swift stream swirls and curls deep below. Continuing through old farmlands for about a quarter mile, we saw tiger lilies, daisies, and other spring flowers before the trail began its woodland climb up a soft-footed, pine-strewn pathway to the top of Pine Mountain at Scott Gap. The trail is quiet, scenic, and peaceful but presents a steep and strenuous pull.

At Scott Gap at 2.5 miles, the trail intersects Hannah Mountain Trail, a long trail starting beyond Cades Cove on Parson Branch Road to follow the mountain ranges to the Abrams Creek area. Still following directions for the loop walk, we turned left on Hannah Mountain Trail to discover a delightful fairy-tale walk through a cool, deep, virgin forest with many tree trunks 24-30 inches in diameter. We saw a large variety of mushrooms and deep-woods wildflowers scattered amid lush ferns. Mountain rills spilled out of the hillsides in gurgling rivulet waterfalls to drop into clear little pools. The trail gradually descends through a dense forest of hardwoods, pines, and hemlocks before it drops down an abrupt ridge section to Abrams Creek. The water thunders down the mountain between two sharp and rocky hillsides, but there are no big rocks or a footbridge to cross on. The wide stream was too swift and deep to consider navigating that June day, so we turned to retrace our 4.3 miles hike up the Hannah Mountain Trail and down the Rabbit Creek Trail back to our car.

Big Creek Trail

Date Hiked: SUMMER - June 14th
Mileage: 5.6 miles Roundtrip
Our Rating: Moderate
Directions: I-40 to NC to exit 451 at Waterville; cross bridge and turn left; continue on 5.7 miles straight to the Big Creek picnic area and parking lot.

Trail Description:

The Big Creek Trail, beginning 0.2 mile past the Ranger Station and just before the Big Creek Picnic Area, follows an old logging road rising up the creek valley between Mount Cammerer and Mount Sterling. Containing several hiking trails, the Big Creek area on the northeastern boundary of the Park was a totally new section of the Smokies for us to visit and explore on a hot day in mid June. We chose the creekside trail because mountain streams in the Smokies, usually 50 degrees, actually cool or air-condition the trail areas around them.

The trail travels on a wide, well-marked dirt roadbed that was once an old Indian trail across the mountains and later a logging and motor route. In the first half mile, the pathway rises away from the creek to cross over a hill, with glimpses of the ridgelines of Mount Sterling through the trees, before dropping again to follow alongside the stream for the rest of the hike. Big Creek is a beautiful, broad, rumbling, and noisy stream. The cold mountain water splashes and spills over giant boulders, offering hikers continuous shows of small waterfalls chasing over creek rocks and boulders.

The Midnight Hole

Following a gradual ascent uphill along the banks of Big Creek, the trail moves through a diverse forest of maples, tulip poplars, sycamores, hemlocks, and rhododendron. Sometimes the way is rocky and rough underfoot. At 1 mile, look for the foundations of an old stone shelter to the right of the trail, called the Rock House, and at 1.4 miles, stop to enjoy a spot the locals call the Midnight Hole. Families often picnic and swim here where the creek spills over in a 6-foot falls to a wide, dark green pool. This trail is beautiful at every point with the continuing displays of mountain cascades and large rocks along the way. A little farther up the trail at 2.1 miles, walk to the left on a short side path to see Mouse Creek Falls, a side tributary spilling in a 50-foot cascade down a rock bank into Big Creek. Continuing on, the trail turns left over a long footbridge crossing of Big Creek at 2.2 miles. Take a break on the rocks below the bridge and look for mountain trout in the water.

Beyond the bridge, the pathway narrows as it rises along the side of the stream, continuing toward Cosby Knob. Watch for two large boulders along the path at 2.4 miles; and shortly after, at 3 miles, look for a long series of rivulets running down a rock wall along the trailside to the left called Brakeshoe Spring. The name Brakeshoe comes from a railcar accident that once occurred here, and the spring is a good place to turn back for a 6 miles roundtrip day hike.

Mouse Creek Falls

77

Lower Mount Cammerer

Date Hiked: SUMMER - June 26th
Mileage: 5 miles Roundtrip
Our Rating: Moderate
Directions: I-40 to Exit 443 at Foothills Parkway; follow Parkway onto Hwy 321/32, staying on Hwy 32 to road to Cosby Campground; follow road 3 miles to picnic area, park and walk past amphitheater to trailhead on left.

Trail Description:

Guidebooks describe this trail as an easy "stroll" wandering gently around the lowlands of Mount Cammerer, but this is not a very accurate description. Instead, the trail rolls up and down the ridges in a roller-coaster fashion, climbing from the campground to Sutton Ridge at 1.5 miles, down Sutton Ridge, and then up and down over Gilliland Ridge, Leadmine Ridge, and Rowdy Ridge before finally arriving at Campsite #35 at 3.5 miles and on to the Appalachian Trail at the trail's end at 7.5 miles.

To get to the trailhead, walk up the campground road past the ampitheater and turn left on the trail marked Appalachian Trail/Sutton Ridge. Follow

ahead approximately a quarter mile to a trail intersection, where Low Gap Trail turns right and a nature trail angles left. Lower Mount Cammerer Trail continues straight on an ample roadbed that winds uphill through hemlocks, hardwoods, and dogwoods. It crosses several tributaries before coming to an open

turnaround at one half mile. You may see remnants of an old stone wall shortly after this point, a reminder of the settlers who once made their homes in this area. The trail soon comes within sound and sight of Toms Creek, navigating it over rocks at 0.8 mile and crossing a second tributary of the creek over a foot log at 1 mile. This pretty stream is a nice place to stop and rest.

Mount Cammerer Trail then leads more steeply upward for 0.5 mile to Sutton Ridge, a good lunch spot at 1.5 miles along the way. A marked side trail leads 200 yards to a fine overlook with views of Gabes Mountain and the Cosby Valley. After rising to Sutton Ridge, the trail now descends down the other side of the ridge, angling right, to wind around the lower ridgelines of Mount Cammerer. The trail along several of the lower areas in late June was overgrown with high grasses and stickery blackberry branches. There were early summer wildflowers along the trailside including Indian cucumber, blue cohosh, and yellow buttercups.

At approximately 2 miles, the trail crosses Riding Fork Creek. Look upstream here to see the water rippling down several levels of mossy steps, with wild sedum growing along the banks. We turned around at about 2.5 miles after climbing up Gilliland Ridge. Another mile's hike would have taken us uphill again, over another ridgetop, and then finally down to Campsite #35 at 3.5 miles. On another day when we hiked this trail, we took the full 7 miles roundtrip hike to Campsite #35 and back. After returning to the Cosby Campground, we cooked hot dogs and chili and enjoyed the added treat of listening to a local bluegrass band.

Bote Mountain Trail

Date Hiked: SUMMER - August 3nd
Mileage: 8.4 miles Roundtrip
Our Rating: Moderate - Strenuous
Directions: Hwy 321 to Townsend Wye; right on Laurel Creek
Road for 4.4 miles; parking is on right; trailhead is on left.

Trail Description:

The Bote Mountain Trail is the remains of the Bote Mountain Road that
went up and over the mountain to North Carolina. Notice the word up in that
description. This uphill journey, with some very steep pump-up-your-heartbeat

stretches, is a popular
route to get to Spence
Field, a grassy bald on
the Appalachian Trail.
The hike of approxi-
mately 7.2 miles up
Bote Mountain Trail
to the Appalachian
Trail and Spence Field
is strenuous for most
people.

After parking
at the Schoolhouse
Gap parking pullover,
walk about 250 yards up the road to the Bote Mountain trailhead on the left.
The first 4.2 miles of the trail we explored basically has two sections. The first
1.2 miles rise gradually west and uphill from the road through a green forest

and rhododendron
tunnels. A shallow,
narrow rill trickles
downhill to the right
of the path. This first
part of the trail is a
soft, though continu-
ally uphill, pathway.
At 1.2 miles, Bote
Mountain Trail turns
sharply right at an
intersection, with
the West Prong Trail

turning left. From this point the old roadbed broadens out and rises south up the slope of Bote Mountain Ridge.

On this second section, following the ridgeline of Bote Mountain, you will encounter many open areas to the left with vistas of Defeat Ridge, Thunderhead, and the Smokies ranges. At 1.8 miles Finley Cane Trail intersects on the right. After this point Bote Mountain Trail grows progressively steeper and rockier underfoot, for more difficult hiking, as the trail rises about 800 feet in one mile. The forest is not very scenic in this area, making the walk more boring and tedious. At approximately 2.5 miles, watch for a big log on the left for a welcome spot to rest and enjoy a backpack lunch.

The sharp ascent finally lessens and mellows out for a short stretch before beginning to climb even more sharply once again as Bote Mountain continues to rise to the Appalachian Trail high above. Settlers once herded cattle up this trail to the green pastures at Spence Field, and it is hard to imagine how they managed to move them up this steep trek. We hiked to the intersection of Lead Cove Trail at 4.2 miles that hot day in August and then turned around to head back. If you are game for a longer hike, continue to the junction of Forney Creek Trail at 5.5 miles, or on to the trail's end at its junction with the Appalachian Trail at 7.2 miles. The return hike is, gratefully, all downhill.

Old Settlers Trail

Date Hiked: SUMMER - August 9th
Mileage: 7 miles Roundtrip
Our Rating: Moderate
Directions: Hwy 441 to Gatlinburg; left on Hwy 321 at Traffic Light #3; right at 6 miles on Greenbrier Road; drive 3.2 miles to bridge to Ramsey Cascades Trail; trail is on the left just across the bridge; use pullover parking on roadside.

Trail Description:

  Old Settlers Trail is one of those delightful but seldom hiked trails in the Smokies. Perhaps it gets overlooked because the well-known Ramsey Cascades Trail is nearby; most people just zoom by the Old Settlers trailhead on the way to Ramsey Cascades. Beginning on the left just after the bridge crossing over the Little Pigeon River, Old Settlers Trail travels north parallel with the river and then angles right to start a winding journey into the cove and around the baseline of the Greenbrier Pinnacle. For the first half mile, you are never far from the Little Pigeon River, which you can often hear to your left. Soft underfoot, the path wanders through an open woods, following beside or crossing various creek branches. There are more than six stream crossings in the 3.5 miles trail section we walked. Most crossings are only as wide as a sidewalk, but all are picturesque.

  The winding path crosses Bird Branch at 0.3 mile, and then over a little ridge is another stream crossing at 0.5 mile. The footpath then angles right on a

pleasant lowland trail, twining along woodsy, green hillsides and then dropping down to small, pretty stream crossings. In spring many varieties of wildflowers grow along Old Settlers Trail; and even in August, although late for most flowers, we still saw patches of yellow tickseed, blue asters, goldenrod, and plantain spires. Several times the pathway moved through open field areas where the meadow grass grew knee-high in early August, often making hiking more difficult. The tall grass reminded us that many settlers once lived in this Greenbrier valley area, and as we walked along, we saw an occasional rock wall or open clearing that hinted of these early settlements. Later in the hike, we found more stone chimneys, fences, and bits of foundations of old homes and walls along the trailside.

At approximately 1.2 miles, the trail skips over Little Bird Branch and follows the creek before angling left and starting to climb up the side of the Cope-

land Divide. The trail grows steeper as it climbs along the ridgelines. At approximately 2 miles the pathway drops to cross Copeland Creek and then rises again to snake around the ridgelines before dropping to a crossing of Snakefeeder Branch at 3 miles.

The trail now follows along the stream for a short distance with pretty cascades along the way. We turned around after another rise in the trail and a crossing of Soak Ash Creek at 3.5 miles. Further up the trail you will find the remnants of old settlers' homesites and a still-standing rock chimney if you want to walk on. The Old Settlers Trail is a wonderful Smokies trail you shouldn't miss.

Twentymile Trail

Date Hiked: SUMMER - September 6th
Mileage: 6 miles Roundtrip
Our Rating: Moderate
Directions: Hwy 321 from Maryville to right over Foothills Parkway; left on Hwy 129, then left on NC Hwy 28 for 3 miles to left at Twentymile sign; park at end of road.

Trail Description:

       The Twentymile trailhead is approximately one and one-half hours from Knoxville on the North Carolina side of the Smokies. The drive over the mountain to the trailhead weaves down snakelike Hwy 129 through Deals Gap. Watch carefully for the entrance to Twentymile off Highway 28; it is easy to miss. After the Twentymile turn, drive up the access road past the unused ranger station to park. Walk behind the gate onto an old logging roadbed, which is the start of the trail. Twentymile is a moderately ascending trail traveling 3 miles up a stream valley to Proctor Field Gap and then another 1.7 miles to the trail's end at Sassafras Gap on Shuckstack Mountain.

       The trail walks through a shady hardwood and pine forest on its journey to Proctor Field Gap, but the cool streams and tumbling water are what make this trail so special. There are large rocky shelves on the trailside and giant boulders in the streams. Lood for white quartz in the rocks on the trailside and sometimes you might find quartz chunks along the pathway you can pick up and examine.

The first mile of the trail is the most hiked since it leads to Twentymile Cascades. The broad path follows Moore Springs Branch on the right and crosses over the stream on a bridge at 0.5 mile. After crossing the bridge, the Wolf Ridge Trail branches to the left and Twentymile Trail angles and continues to the right. A spur trail on the right just after this point leads approximately 100 yards down to the Twentymile Cascades, where Twentymile Creek tumbles down into Moore Springs Branch in a series of rushing waterfalls over several stair-step boulders.

After walking down the short spur and back to the main pathway, Twentymile Trail continues climbing the creek valley between the high points of Shuckstack Mountain to the right and Gregory Bald to the left. The hike is an uphill march from this point on, strenuous in many spots, moderate in others. The trail follows the stream, crisscrossing it several times as it rises up to the Gap. You will enjoy the many waterfalls, moss-covered boulders, and scenic spots on this backwoods exploration. Twentymile Campsite #93 comes into view at 1.8 miles, soon followed by another bridge crossing. Watch for a long rock slide in the creek after this point. The last two bridges before the junction are at 2.5 and 2.6 miles. At 3 miles you reach Proctor Field Gap, a wide area in the old roadway where two other trails intersect. This is a nice turnaround point.

Twentymile Cascades

Meigs Creek Trail

Date Hiked: SUMMER - September 12th
Mileage: 7 miles Roundtrip
Our Rating: Strenuous
Directions: Hwy 321 from Maryville to the Townsend Wye; left on Little River Road 6 miles to The Sinks parking lot on right; trailhead starts behind The Sinks.

Trail Description:

Plan to hike Meigs Creek Trail when the weather has been dry a few weeks in the Smokies and when the creeks are down. The trail crosses back and forth over picturesque Meigs Creek eighteen to twenty times on its 3.5 miles journey up to intersect with the Lumber Ridge Trail and Meigs Mountain Trail. There are no footbridges, and if the water is high you may find the crossings difficult to achieve without getting your feet wet.

The trail begins behind an area the locals call The Sinks, where the Little River spills down over a ledge into a deep, wide pool between high rocky ledges. The popular pool draws a crowd of divers and swimmers in warm weather, and the parking lot is often full in summer, so fall or spring may be a better time for hiking this trail. At the back of the parking area on the right, follow the rocky stairs and path that climb up the ledges behind the Sinks. The trail then follows high above and parallel with Little River for about a quarter mile before switching back sharply to the left along a high, narrow ridgeline of Curry He Mountain. Here you wind in a gradual descent down the mountain-

A cold refreshing swim at the Sinks

side. This dry, south-facing slope is an attractive area for snakes. We encountered a large snake sprawled in the sun directly across the trail and two more snakes farther up the trail in the same day. Likely, there is a popular pit for snakes in this area, so be very cautious about your footing on this trail.

Coming down off the ridgeline at 1 mile, Meigs Creek Trail begins to meander through a rhododendron tunnel, into a forest, and along the banks of tumbling Meigs Creek. Here you commence a back-and-forth journey of stream crossings. Usually there are rocks and boulders to hop your way over at each creek junction. The trail is narrow, often strewn with pine needles, and soft under foot. The woods along the creek are lush, green, and shady. After the fourth stream crossing, the path narrows between rocky valley walls and the creekside. Watch for a pretty 10 foot cascade plunging down over a rocky ledge at approximately 1.8 miles.

There are many broad, very tall trees along the trail now, including a huge beech at 2 miles and some vast hemlocks farther up the way. Several side branches and tributaries spill down to angle into Meigs Creek after 2.5 miles, including Bloody Branch, Henderson, Bunch, and Curry Prong. The trail grows steeper in the last mile, while Meigs Creek and its crossings become more narrow. At 3.5 miles the trail ends at an open, turn-around junction.

Twin Creeks Trail

Date Hiked: SUMMER - September 20th
Mileage: 5 miles Roundtrip
Our Rating: Easy - Moderate
Directions: Hwy 441 into Gatlinburg; left on Airport Road at Traffic Light #8 to Cherokee Orchard Road to trailhead on right just past Park Boundary signs.
Trail Description:

Many hikers miss knowing about Twin Creeks Trail because the beginning of the trail is easy to miss and few hiking guides include accounts describing this nice walk. Twin Creeks Trail meanders 2 miles through the woodland, parallel to Cherokee Orchard Road, to end at a short connecting trail that intersects with the Ogle Nature Trail behind the Noah "Bud" Ogle cabin. Adding the nature loop to the overall journey brings the round-trip total of this hike to 5 miles.

The Twin Creeks Trail starts just inside the park boundary one block past the entrance to Mynatt Park. You will find the trail sign on the right side of Cherokee Orchard Road with a small parking area across the street from the sign. After parking and walking across the road, follow the pathway behind the trail sign. It weaves into the woods and then turns left at the creek. You can see a row of quaint mountain cottages across the stream on LeConte Road. After angling left, Twin Creeks Trail follows a gentle ascending pathway through the open woods. The walk is pleasant on this early section of this trail, winding through hardwoods and hemlocks beside the creek. As you walk on, Twin Creeks Trail moves into

deeper forest, often skirting Le Conte Creek or crossing it, and frequently weaving within sight and sound of Cherokee Orchard Road.

At approximately 0.6 mile, the path crosses a narrow, paved road, leading 300 yards to the left to Cherokee Orchard Road. A short walk to the right takes you to the new Twin Creeks Science and Education Center, a beautiful research and education facility opened in 2007. To continue on the Twin Creeks Trail, walk directly across the road, following right along an old stone wall. Turn left into the Science Center road and look for the trail sign on left. The pathway continues again into the woods, winding gradually uphill through more hardwoods and hemlocks. Signs of old homesites, rock walls, clearings, and chimney remains abound along the way, reminding you of the many settlers who once lived in this area of the mountains not far from Gatlinburg.

Midway along, the pathway crosses Twin Creek over the rocks to pick up on the other side. At ap-proximately 2 miles the trail ends with no marker, but an ongoing pathway clearly continues. This path ends shortly into the nature trail running from behind the Ogle cabin. Turn left to the cabin or right to take the three-quarter-mile Noah "Bud" Ogle Nature Trail, a picturesque walk that loops through the woods in a gentle circle before coming out near the back of the Ogle cabin. You can walk around the historic site, explore the inside of an old farmhouse and eat lunch on the covered back porch before you start the easy, downhill return to your car.

Gold Mine Trail

Date Hiked: FALL - September 26th
Mileage: 6 miles Roundtrip
Our Rating: Strenuous - Moderate
Directions: Hwy 321 from Maryville to right on Foothills Parkway; drive 9 miles to left on Flats Road; stay right at campground entrance and follow Flats Road left into Top of the World Community at sign; at 2 miles turn right on Jouroulman Drive into Park Lane Heights; take first right on Steffner Circle; unmarked trailhead on right of road at 0.1 mile; park on left in pullover.

Trail Description:

Gold Mine's name comes from the fact that gold was panned briefly but unsuccessfully from this area of the mountains. The trailhead is difficult to find, and unless you know the area, you might get lost. We did get lost the first time—and we live here. Gold Mine Trail branches out of the back of a small community of homes at the edge of the National Park boundary. There are no directional markers from Foothills Parkway and no sign to look for directly on the road where the trail starts. An incentive for finding the Gold Mine Trail, besides wanting to explore and enjoy it for itself, is to gain a more direct access to

the Cooper Road Trail and other trails branching off of it. Accessing these trails via Gold Mine Trail can cut several miles off future hiking trips to Beard Cane Trail and Cane Creek Trail.

Gold Mine is a predominantly steep and rocky hike connecting the Cooper Road to the southwest National Park boundary at the base of Chilhowee Mountain. After parking on Steffner Circle, look for the beginning of the trail on the right side of the road. Walk down a dirt pathway, past a horse barn on the left, and then into the woods. You will see the Park boundary sign for Gold Mine Trail at 0.2 mile. There is an open area here before the trail starts its descent into the park. A neighborly hound dog, that we nicknamed Bubba, joined us at this point and walked with us the entire hike.

The ongoing trail is an old dirt roadbed, rutted out in many places, and very rock-strewn. It is a trek most all the way, often difficult under foot, with few scenic stretches. There is a rhododendron tunnel in the early section of the trail and an area or two with shady woods. You will see a diversity of rock here, sandstone, shale, quartzite, and maybe a deceptive glitter of gold! At 1 mile Gold Mine Trail ends at Gold Mine Gap in a broad intersection with the Cooper Road. This wider pathway travels 11 miles from Abrams Campground to Cades Cove.

After a rest on logs at the intersection, we turned left to extend our hike along a stretch of the Cooper Road. The trail descended through a pretty forest of hardwoods for a half-mile before arriving at the trailhead of Cane Creek Trail. It then rose uphill 1.2 more miles to the intersection of Beard Cane Trail. We turned around, a half mile further, at a scenic ridge at 3 miles, having enjoyed the fall foliage and the colored leaves all along the Cooper Road. Our return hike was more strenuous than the hike in, especially the sharp climb back up the Gold Mine Trail. Even the hound dog was panting and ready for a drink.

A thirsty friend we met on the trail

91

Cane Creek Trail

Date Hiked: FALL - October 4th
Mileage: 7.2 miles Roundtrip
Our Rating: Moderate - Strenuous
Directions: Hwy 321 from Maryville to right on Foothills Parkway; drive 9 miles to left on Flats Road; stay right at campground entrance and follow Flats Road left into Top of the World Community at sign; at 2 miles turn right on Jouroulman Drive into Park Lane Heights; take first right on Steffner Circle; unmarked trailhead on right of road at 0.1 mile; park on left in pullover.

Trail Description:

Having found a shorter access route to Cane Creek Trail in September via the Gold Mine Trail, we returned in October to explore the Cane Creek Trail. As before, we drove to the Gold Mine trailhead, hiked that trail 1 mile down to Gold Mine Gap, and then another half mile to the left on Cooper Road to the Cane Creek trailhead. At 1.5 miles at Cane Gap, the Cane Creek Trail drops steeply to the left toward the Cane Creek lowlands. Note that word "steeply." The first half mile travels down a very sharp incline as it begins to drop toward the bottomland below. The single file path then descends more gradually until it reaches a low creek valley lying between the bases of Hatcher Mountain and Chilhowee Mountain.

The ongoing path, now broader, winds its way into the Cane Creek valley to arrive at Campsite #2 at 0.7 mile from the start of the trailhead. This appealing but little-used campsite is a quiet, restful place to pause and enjoy the woods setting and the picturesque views along the creekside. Beyond the campsite, the trail travels in an almost straight line, always following near Cane

Creek. There are two crisscrosses of the creek shortly after the campsite and several later crossings of little tributaries.

In October, the first time we hiked this trail, fall leaves were strewn among the pine-needles all over the forest floor and path. On a second hike in spring, the lowlands were scattered with wildflowers in a lush, green atmosphere. This trail is always pretty.

The last section of the trail stretching to the end of Cane Creek Trail is a continuing delight as you walk through a fairies-and-elves woodland with Cane Creek babbling along the way. On our hike we saw a beautiful variety of trees, shrubs, mosses, and ferns, as well as many kinds of mushrooms, includling fairy

rings of small white mushrooms underneath the trees. This entire valley area was once Buchanan farmland, and you will find their small family cemetery at 1.5 miles.

Beyond the cemetery, the trail thins to an abrupt end at the Park boundary at 2.1 miles from the trailhead, where you turn to start the journey back.

Note: this trail would not be a good choice to hike after heavy rains, as the creek here rises and spreads, making the bottomland slushy or sometimes flooding.

93

Little Cataloochee Trail

Date Hiked: FALL - October 18th
Mileage: 6.2 miles Roundtrip
Our Rating: Moderate
Directions: I-40 to NC Exit 20; 0.2 mile on Route 276 to right on Cove Creek Road, follow this narrow, gravel road over the mountain to intersection with paved road; turn left into the Cataloochee Valley; 5.5 miles to pullover parking on left at trailhead.

Trail Description:

This delightful trail wanders through an old settlement area, but getting to the trailhead is a bit of an adventure. The trip from the Knoxville area to the Cataloochee Valley will take you at least an hour and a half. Cove Creek Road (old Hwy 284) becomes a narrow, dirt road as it climbs over Cataloochee Divide and down into the valley, where the paved road into Cataloochee Valley turns left. Stay straight on Cove Creek for 5.5 miles, following the unpaved road until you arrive at the trail sign for Little Cataloochee on the left side of the road. The drive to Cataloochee and through the valley is beautiful in the fall when the colors are at their peak. Cataloochee Valley is much like Cades Cove, but is lesser known and doesn't draw as much traffic and tourism.

Little Cataloochee Trail begins at an old gate. The old settlers' roadbed travels briefly downhill before beginning a rolling journey up and down in and out of the lower ridges of Mount Sterling on the north and the smaller Noland Mountain to the south. At 0.9 mile, Long Bunk

Little Cataloochee Baptist Church - built 1889

Trail intersects from the right as Little Cataloochee winds on to the left through a scenic woods. The trail has some slightly strenuous stretches as it climbs the ridgelines, but then it moderates as it flattens out or falls again. At approximately 1.2 miles look for a side trail to the right to the John Jackson Hannah Cabin built in 1864. The park service has restored it, and you should stop there for a rest on the front porch. Beside the cabin is an old apple tree, and

we found crisp, sweet apples to sample on our October hike.

Back on the main trail, the pathway curves and reaches a bridge crossing of Little Cataloochee Creek at 1.5 miles. After this point the old road ascends up and around a

John Jackson Hannah Cabin

ridge to arrive at Little Cataloochee Baptist Church at 2.1 miles. This is a nice place to have lunch under a shade tree or on the church steps. The white church and its little cemetery are well-maintained, and you can walk inside the sanctuary to see the old wood pews and pulpit. We walked on another mile beyond the

church, passing through old fields and shady forest land, before turning around at 3.1 miles where the trail started to rise sharply to Davidson Gap. For a longer hike, you can climb to the gap and then downhill again to the trail's end at Pretty Hollow Gap Trail at 5.2 miles.

Caldwell Fork Trail

Date Hiked: FALL - October 25th
Mileage: 6.6 miles Roundtrip
Our Rating: Easy - Moderate
Directions: I-40 to NC Exit 20; 0.2 mile on Route 276 to right on Cove Creek Road; follow this narrow, gravel road over the mountain to intersection with paved road; turn left into the Cataloochee Valley; drive 3 miles to pullover parking on left after campground.

Trail Description:

Having discovered the Cataloochee valley earlier in October, we re-

turned one pretty fall day to hike another of its trails. If you love trails by the mountain streams, you will love Caldwell Fork Trail, but if you don't like scenic log footbridges, you probably will not like this trail.

Skirting constantly along the creek banks through a lowland woods and winding back and forth over picturesque mountain streams, Caldwell Fork Trail starts just beyond the Cataloochee campground on the left. The hike first crosses

high over the Cataloochee Creek on a 25-foot long, hewn-log footbridge, one of the longest footbridges in the Smoky Mountains. It is a long drop from the middle of this bridge down to the swift, tumbling stream below. There are 16 more footbridges and one creek crossing over rocks on the next

96

3.3 miles of this trail until it intersects with the McKee Branch Trail. The footbridges, long and short, high and low, cross and recross Caldwell Fork Creek and its multiple tributaries, including Den Branch, Palmer Branch, Sag Branch, Snake Branch, and McKee Branch.

CALDWELL FORK TRAIL
Great Smoky Mtns

After crossing the first footbridge over Cataloochee Creek, Caldwell Fork Trail swings right to soon follow along Caldwell Creek. The trail gradually ascends, seldom becoming strenuous or overly steep as it winds its way upstream, wide enough for a settler's wagon or for two people to walk together. It is also a horse trail, so you have to watch your step for horse piles. If possible, don't take this trail after frequent rains, or you will also find yourself picking your way around many mud quagmires in areas where the horses have mucked up the trail.

The forest along the way is diverse with a variety of hardwoods, pines, hemlocks, Fraser magnolias, mountain laurel, and rhododendron. One of the pleasures of this hike are the many beautiful cascades and pools you see as you follow the creek side. At approximately 1 mile, you will pass the first junction of Boogerman Trail on the left, the other arriving about 2 miles later. At 3.2 miles, Big Fork Ridge Trail angles off to the right, and at 3.3 miles you arrive at the intersection of McKee Branch Trail, which is a good turnaround point. The return hike is all downhill and very easy. You will enjoy this unique trail.

Sugarland Mountain Trail

Date Hiked: FALL - November 1st
Mileage: 6.2 miles Roundtrip
Our Rating: Strenuous
Directions: Hwy 441 through Gatlinburg to Sugarlands Visitor Center; right on Little River Road for 3.7 miles to Laurel Falls parking; trailhead on left.

Trail Description:

The Sugarland Mountain Trail is worth its steep climbs in autumn when the colors are peaking on the Smoky Mountain ranges. This trail is little traveled, so don't let the cars and the multitudes of tourists at the parking area at Fighting Creek Gap fool you. Ninety-nine percent of the people or more are walking up the paved trail to Laurel Falls on the right. The Sugarland trail starts from the other side of the road at the park trail sign.

The first mile angles left up a north ridge of Sugarland Mountain. You can see the trail rising up the hillside through a somewhat open forest, with many pine and hemlock trees. The narrow, single-file path winds uphill strenuously with little relief. In the first 0.5 mile it crosses two scanty streams trickling down the hillside, levels off briefly at 0.6 mile, and then climbs sharply once again. At 1 mile the trail levels out enough for you to finally catch your breath. It then travels across a ridge before starting a sharp descent to arrive at Mids Gap at approximately 1.5 miles. There is an open area in the trail here where an old, unmaintained trail juts right toward the Elkmont area. Sugarland

rolls on to the left through a beautiful woodland of maples, poplars, oaks, elm, beech, sweetgum, birch, and other varieties of hardwoods. The day we hiked, the trees were all ablaze in yellow, orange, and red foliage, with the colorful leaves also thick underfoot in a collage of autumn colors.

The trail begins to rise again after the gap, although not as steeply as at the beginning, and curves sharply right in a switchback to walk out along the ridgetop. At 2.3 miles a clearing offers an incredible vista of Mount Le Conte, the Bullhead, and a host of other mountain ranges. This is a good place to take some memorable photos of the Smokies ranges dressed in their full, brilliant fall colors. The trail continues along this ridgeline section and offers many open points that have other sweeping views of the mountains to the left of the trail. It is worth the climb to see these panoramas. At 3.1 miles the path arrives at a trail junction where Huskey Gap leads left, Little River right, and Sugarland Mountain straight ahead. This is a good turnaround point. You can lunch here or at one of the ridgeline views on your way back down.

If you are hardy enough to hike another mile, you will reach Campsite #21 at 4.1 miles, now closed for camping, but still a nice spot to hike to. The area is strewn with big boulders by a small stream with many wildlflowers in spring.

Rabbit Creek Trail - Cades

Date Hiked: FALL - November 15th
Mileage: 5 miles Roundtrip
Our Rating: Strenuous
Directions: Hwy 321 to Townsend Wye; right on Laurel Creek Road into the Cades Cove loop; turn right after approximately 4.5 miles on road to Abrams Falls; park at the end of the road in parking lot; look for Rabbit Creek trail sign.

Trail Description:

Most people who park at Abrams Falls parking lot are heading to the falls or possibly over to the Elijah Oliver cabin on Wet Bottoms Trail. Both of these trails, as well as Rabbit Creek, start from out of this same Cades Cove area. The sign for Rabbit Creek Trail is to the left of the broad, well-traveled trail to Abrams Falls.

Rabbit Creek Trail begins by following to the left along Mill Creek for a short distance, angling right, and then deadending into the creek. Look across Mill Creek and you will see the trail wandering merrily away again on the other side. The creek is quite wide, and with no bridges to cross or rocks to jump, the only way over is to wade. We pulled off our boots and socks, tied our shoes around our neck, rolled up our pants legs, and took the challenge. Brrrr! We advise doing this trail in the summertime!

Beautiful Cades Cove

Cove Trailhead

After crossing the creek, the trail leads up a wide path hugging a ridgeline along Boring Ridge. The path soon narrows and grows steep and rocky. It walks directly through a streambed much of the time, sometimes with trickles of water running between the rocks. Little rills appear in several places alongside the path.

After over half a mile of strenuous climbing, Rabbit Creek Trail levels out over the top of Boring Ridge. Here the trail moves into a prettier woods thick with pine and hemlock, and the path becomes pine-strewn and soft. Too soon the trail winds uphill steeply again toward Coon Butt. When you reach this high point, a flat ridge walk continues for a mile with vistas and sunny picnic sites. We heard and saw many birds but did not see another hiker on the trail. Our guess is the initial creek wade scares most potential hikers away. After a nice walk across the ridges beyond Coon Butt, the trail starts a somewhat steep descent at 2.3 miles.

The trail is a rather strenuous one, so we only hiked a little piece downhill from Coon Butt, turning around to start our return hike at 2.5 miles. At 4.1 miles after a continual drop, the trail will come to a crossing of Rabbit Creek for which the trail was named and to Rabbit Creek Campsite #15. The ongoing trail rises again after the campsite to meet the Hannah Mountain Trail in approximately one more mile at Scott Gap.

Brrr! A cold crossing of Mill Creek

101

Rainbow Falls

Date Hiked: FALL - November 21st
Mileage: 5.4 miles Roundtrip
Our Rating: Strenuous
Directions: Hwy 441 into Gatlinburg; left on Airport Road at Traffic Light #8; continue onto Cherokee Orchard Road approximately 3.3 miles to trailhead before beginning of the one-way Roaring Fork Motor Nature Trail; parking area and sign on right.

Trail Description:

This trail, a popular route to Mount Le Conte, the third highest peak in the Smokies, is better known as the route to Rainbow Falls, and the parking lot is

often full. The trailhead begins about 2.5 miles past the Park boundary on the Roaring Fork Motor Nature Trail. Rainbow Falls Trail rises continually up the back side of Mount Le Conte for 6 miles to intersect with the Bullhead Trail just 0.6 mile below the Le Conte Lodge and summit.

The hike to the falls is tough for the average person. The steep uphill climb of 2.7 miles can be strenuous for those who seldom walk or hike. The trail rises 1,500 feet in the 2.7 miles to Rainbow Falls. The path has been worn down from many hikers, leaving exposed roots, and you have to carefully watch your footing. The trail also includes several series of rock stairsteps to clamber

up, along with many large boulders to climb around. On the plus side, the trail is very scenic and the waterfall is a memorable one.

Rainbow Falls Trail starts to the right of the parking area, moving into an open forest area on a wide pathway. You soon pass a side path that leads over to the Bullhead Trail.

Then the woods deepen, and the trail narrows and begins to follow along to the left of Le Conte Creek as it cascades and tumbles down from Mount Le Conte. The trail winds its way up through a beautiful forest and out along sunny ridgelines, passing through sweeps of rhododendron and laurel and alongside large rocky boulders. Sometimes the trailway is very rock strewn, but the large rocks beside the path are nice to rest on as you climb. After the first half mile, the trail curves left away from the creek to wind up over a ridge and then back down to the creek again.

At 1.5 miles, you will cross a footbridge over Le Conte Creek and later two small tributaries, one with a small falls. The trail then winds away from the stream to climb a second ridge, before descending back to the creek near the falls. At 2.5 miles, the trail crosses the first of two log bridges as you arrive at the base of the waterfall. Rainbow Falls cascades down 80 feet over a broad, rocky face. There are many big rocks to lunch on at the base of the falls before starting the easier hike back.

Rainbow Falls

Bradley Fork Trail

Date Hiked: FALL - December 6th
Mileage: 7 miles Roundtrip
Our Rating: Easy - Moderate
Directions: Hwy 441 up to Newfound Gap and over mountain into NC to Smokemont Campground; turn left over bridge and left to back of campground to trailhead.
Trail Description:

Bradley Fork, a wonderful family hiking trail, follows an old logging road along the Bradley Fork, a branch of the Oconaluftee River. There are some ups and downs, but this trail is a predominantly gradual and easy walk in its journey up the stream. In winter, the back of Smokemont Campground is often gated, and you may have to hike in a short distance to the trailhead.

Rolling from open woodlands to higher deep forest terrain, the trail travels alongside the Bradley Fork from being a broad, nearly quiet lowland creek until it becomes a rushing, churning mountain stream, tumbling and cascading over huge boulders. This change makes the hike especially memorable. We found ourselves constantly stopping to enjoy the stream, its waterfalls, cascades, pools, and beauty. In the first mile, the path passes several side trails connecting to the area water tower and horse stable but then moves away from signs of civilization. The trail is broad and soft underfoot in most sections and not too rutted, rocky, or steep. The trail often rises up little ridges above the creek, but even in these sections you can hear the waters below and look over to the stream views. Most of the benches on the trailway are crumbling or overgrown, but there are many places where you can walk down to the creek to rest on a big rock by the stream if you get tired and need a break.

The trail crosses several scenic bridges along its route. The first is at 1 mile just before the junction to Chasteen Creek Trail 0.2 mile farther on the right. After climbing up and over a short rise, Bradley Fork

Trail comes to the junction of Smokemont Loop trail at 1.7 miles on the left. A long, high, log bridge spans Bradley Fork as Smokemont Loop begins its journey up a high ridge. After walking out on the bridge to enjoy the stream views, return to the Bradley Fork Trail as it continues along the creek through a shady woods.

At 3 miles, a split in the stream creates an island with bridges leading to it. Across the bridge on the island you will find several pretty picnic spots. This is a good turnaround point for a 6-miles round trip. However, if you want to hike a half-mile farther, there is a scenic cascade where Tawya Creek tumbles into the

Bradley Fork. The walk up Bradley Fork Trail to the island is 3 miles, to the cascades 3.5 miles, or to the intersection with Cabins Flats Trail 4.1 miles. The return hike is an all downhill easy return. You can stretch out your stride on this trail, no matter how far you decide to walk.

Lumber Ridge Trail

Date Hiked: FALL - December 6th
Mileage: 6 miles Roundtrip
Our Rating: Moderate - Strenuous
Directions: Hwy 321 to Townsend Wye; right on Laurel Creek Road; first left at 0.2 mile onto Tremont Road; drive 2 miles to Tremont Institute and parking at trailhead.

Trail Description:

There is no trail sign at the Institute parking lot, and the Tremont Institute, which has an information center, bookstore, and restroom, is unfortunately seldom open on weekends when most people can take time to hike. Look for the road rising out of the back of the parking lot and begin your hike there heading west. You will soon see the Lumber Ridge Trail sign on the left. It is a predominantly uphill and strenuous 4 miles hike climbing Lumber Ridge to its end at Buckhorn Gap.

The trail rises out of Tremont to wiggle its way around and to the top of Lumber Ridge along the ridgelines and then on to Buckhorn Gap. The initial section of the trail is a gravel road, but the roadway quickly changes to a single-file logging trail. In the first half mile you can hear, but not see, the Middle Prong River below in the valley, but the trail soon moves away from the stream, weaving right and rolling upward. This area of Tremont was once

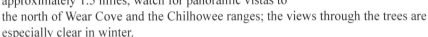

heavily logged, but it is growing back beauti-
fully. There are pine and hardwood trees, and
in winter the silvery white trunks of the birch
trees are lovely against a brilliant blue sky.
The trail crosses a few spring trickles but no
large creeks or streams. It often hugs and hangs
on the vertical sides of Mill Ridge as it rises. At
approximately 1.5 miles, watch for panoramic vistas to
the north of Wear Cove and the Chilhowee ranges; the views through the trees are
especially clear in winter.

The trail reaches a saddle between Lumber and Mill ridges at 2.4 miles.
There is a clearing at this high point with logs for a rest and picnic lunch after the
long climb. The hike to the top of Lumber Ridge is taxing and will pump up your
heart rate. After reaching the saddle, Lumber Ridge Trail then follows out along
the ridge, first descending from the saddle for about 0.5 mile and then flattening
out for the last lap of its journey to Buckhorn Gap. This section of the trail is more
moderate and pleasurable. There are scenic views here and an assortment of wildlife; we saw birds, squirrels, and a grouse. We gathered cones from the pine and
hemlock trees and enjoyed the softer footed trail these trees created. We turned
around at 3 miles, but you may want to continue another mile further to Buckhorn Gap where Meigs Creek and Meigs Mountain trails intersect. The return of
Lumber Ridge is mostly downhill, but keep in mind that it is steep and physically
demanding, too.

Curry Mountain Trail

Date Hiked: WINTER - March 7th
Mileage: 6.6 miles Roundtrip
Our Rating: Moderate - Strenuous
Directions: Hwy 321 from Maryville to Townsend Wye; left on Little River Road 7.7 miles to Metcalf Bottoms parking area; walk up Little River Road 1,000 feet to trailhead on right.
Trail Description:

After the winter holidays and a record-breaking eight weekends of rain and snows in Tennessee, we finally returned to the Smokies trails in early March. We chose peaceful Curry Mountain Trail, which is another of those little known or written-up mountain pathways. Sometimes these are the nicest trails since you seldom see anyone else on the path, giving you more of a sense of adventure, discovery, and quietude as you hike.

Curry Mountain Trail begins on the Little River Road just beyond Metcalf Bottoms. The path skirts first from the road across a grassy, open area and then enters the woods and starts to climb. It follows the remnants of a settlers' path winding upward around the slopes of Curry He and Curry She Mountains. The odd mountain names are taken from Cherokee Indian terms. The trail is uphill with several especially steep inclines, hard on the calves both hiking in and out. We noticed this more so because we had been off the trail for three months. Fortunately, many flatter trail areas, or reliefs, modify the strenuousness of this

trail and make the hike more interesting.

Curry Mountain Trail is a diversified hike, weaving from open to deep forest, often making its way through long rhododendron tunnels and across sparkling, babbling little creeks trickling downhill from the mountains. The first creek is called Breakfast Branch at 0.6

mile. Beyond the creek, the trail moves through a deep, shady evergreen and hemlock grove. As the pathway turns to walk parallel to the road, it passes through a fairy-tale rhododendron tunnel where the trees stretch shady boughs in an

arch over the trail and then on through a stand of mountain laurels. The narrowing roadbed now grows rockier as it ascends, twisting snake-like to arrive at Curry Gap between the Curry He and Curry She mountains at 2 miles. Then the trail switches to the right and left, in and out, along the ridges toward Meigs Mountain. At 2.5 miles we ran into a damaged area where recent storms and high winds had uprooted several trees and thrown them over the trail. We had to scramble over the tree trunks blocking the path.

As the Curry Mountain Trail continues to ascend, many open spots look out to panoramic vistas back down the mountain ranges. The trail ends at 3.3 miles where it intersects Meigs Mountain Trail, having gained over 1,100 feet on the journey. A little cemetery 50 yards to the right is an interesting place to rest before the return.

Hannah Mountain Trail

Date Hiked: SPRING - April 11th
Mileage: 6.4 miles Roundtrip
Our Rating: Easy
Directions: Hwy 321 to Townsend Wye; right on Laurel Creek Road continuing into Cades Cove Loop; first right after Visitor Center on Forge Creek Road and then right on one-way gravel Parson Branch Road 4 miles to trailhead on right.

Trail Description:

Hannah Mountain is a perfect hike for a warm spring day when you want to enjoy an easy, scenic walk back through a quiet forest. The trailhead begins

off the narrow one-way Parson Branch Road out of the back of Cades Cove. Be forewarned that when you finish your hike, you must drive on down Parson Branch Road to come out on the western end of the Smokies on Hwy 129 above Deals Gap. Turn right here and follow 129 back over the mountain and to the Foothills Parkway. The drive on Parson Branch Road is an adventure in itself.

The 9.5-miles-long Hannah Mountain Trail connects Cades Cove to the Abrams Creek area. Each end of the trail has its own distinctive flavor. The

southern end of the trail rolls along gently in and around the hillsides of Hannah Mountain for three full miles before it begins a descent to arrive at Campsite #14 at Flint Gap at 4.5 miles.

The trail begins at a rustic park sign and wanders off to the right in a northwesterly direction for 0.5 mile. The single-file path journeys through pine and hardwood forest land with a soft footing of pine needles much of the way. There are several switchbacks at 0.5 mile before the trail straightens out on the ridgeline again. On our April hike along this trail, many spring plants and wild flowers were popping out: yellow and purple violets, squawroot, chickweed, white bloodroot, and hairy wood betony.

Between 1 mile and 1.5 miles the trail begins walking out on Mount Lanier, the highest point on this Hannah Mountain walk. The woods are often open here with vistas out to the right and left of the mountains and valleys beyond. To the south you can see over into the green valley of Cades Cove with Rich Mountain and Chilhowee rolling up beyond.

We ate our lunch in a grassy area on Mount Lanier where we could look out across one of these fine views.

At 2.3 miles on the right of the trail, stands a giant poplar, 6-7 feet in diameter. Shortly after it, the path narrows to hug a steep ridgeline ahead. At approximately 2.8 miles we were hampered by many large uprooted trees that had fallen over the trail. Soon tired of clambering over tree trunks, we turned around shortly afterwards at 3.2 miles as Hannah Mountain Trail began its long descent toward Flint Gap.

Thomas Divide Trail

Date Hiked: SPRING - April 18th
Mileage: 6.4 miles Roundtrip
Our Rating: Moderate - Strenuous
Directions: Hwy 441 from Gatlinburg up to Newfound Gap and on for 4.4 miles to trail sign and pullover parking on the right of Newfound Gap Road.

Trail Description:

Early spring, before the foliage fills in, is an excellent time to hike Thomas Divide Trail and enjoy all the stunning panoramas of the mountain ranges. The trail starts on Thomas Ridge not far from Newfound Gap, at approximately 4,500 feet elevation, and then climbs the ridgeline to follow a high trail to Nettle Creek Bald at 2.5 miles. The Thomas Divide Trail, 13.8 miles in length from beginning to end, winds its way across several spectacular ridgelines before dropping down the mountainside to end near the Deep Creek campground area at Bryson City, North Carolina.

The first half-mile is mostly uphill, the trail narrow and a little rough with exposed roots to step over. However, even this early section of the trail has several glimpses of Smokies ranges to the right of the pathway to delight you. After reaching an open gap at 0.8 mile, you can rest on a log and look forward to a flatter trail for most of the rest of the way. The trail angles left here to follow the crest of the ridgeline, wandering through a variety of open areas, woods, and rhododendron tunnels. When we hiked in mid April the ground was heavily covered with delicate white spring beauty spreading all along the trailside and under the trees like a floral carpet. Farther on at 1.1 miles, the trail angles right again to curl around Beetree Ridge before arriving at a high point called Turkey Flytrap. Here at an elevation of over 5,000 feet, you will enjoy fine views back up the mountain to

New-found Gap and Mount Kephart. As you continue hiking, you will encounter many more memorable views as the pathway rises to Nettle Creek Bald. We often could see blue mountain ranges spreading out on both sides of this mountaintop trail.

At 1.8 miles, the trail drops to reach a junction with Kanati Fork Trail on the left. Hikers with two vehicles can create a loop hike and walk down Kanati 2.9 miles to a second car. Past the Kanati intersection, Thomas Divide Trail ascends again to follow out across another beautiful Smokies ridgeline.

After undulating up and down, the trailway climbs to the crest of Nettle Creek Bald at 2.8 miles. Although this is the highest point on the hike at 5,160 feet, the bald is too heavily forested to allow good views. We discovered lush green fern and painted trillium on this section of the trail nestled under mixed hardwoods and tall hemlocks. After crossing the forested bald, the winding pathway begins to drop steeply, heading toward Tuskee Gap at 4 miles from the trailhead. We turned around at 3.2 miles as the trail began its descent to the gap.

113

Pretty Hollow Gap Trail

Date Hiked: SPRING - April 25th
Mileage: 5.6 miles Roundtrip
Our Rating: Moderate - Easy
Directions: I-40 to NC Exit 20; 0.2 mile on Route 276 to right on Cove Creek Road; follow this narrow, gravel road over mountain to intersection with paved road, turn left into Cataloochee Valley; approximately 4-5 miles to end of paved road to trail on right.

Trail Description:

Pretty Hollow Gap Trail follows an old settlers' road that travels 5.3 miles from the Cataloochee Valley up along Pretty Hollow Creek to Mount Sterling

ridge high above. The first 2.5 miles progress up an easy-to-moderate ascent, while the last 2.8 miles become increasingly strenuous. An interesting side excursion before you begin your hike is to walk over to the historic Beech Grove School and look through its two restored schoolrooms.

The early portion of the trail, a wide, soft roadbed, is an idyllic hike through open woods along the tumbling waters and cascades of Pretty Hollow Creek. The trail passes a horse camp at 0.2 mile and then begins to ramble along Pretty Hollow Creek on the left.

Watch for a nice waterfall at 0.5 mile spilling over a log in the creek. You will also enjoy looking for wildflowers scattered along the trailside in April. We spotted spring beauties, bloodroot, trout lillies, and trillium. After passing over a gentle rise, Pretty Hollow Gap Trail meets Little Cataloochee

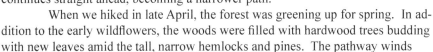

Trail coming in from the right at 0.8 mile. The path then rises up and over another ridge to arrive at the trail intersection with Palmer Creek Trail on the left at 1.3 miles. At the intersection is a scenic spot where Falling Rock Creek tumbles down to converge with Palmer Creek. A log bridge crosses the creek to the left here to follow up Palmer Creek Trail, but Pretty Hollow Gap Trail continues straight ahead, becoming a narrower path.

When we hiked in late April, the forest was greening up for spring. In addition to the early wildflowers, the woods were filled with hardwood trees budding with new leaves amid the tall, narrow hemlocks and pines. The pathway winds

on in an undulating pattern, soon crossing Palmer Creek and then rising sharply to curl along Indian Ridge, no longer following close to the creek. At about 1.5 miles you will spot an especially large tulip tree on the right of the path. The trail then descends to Campsite #39 at 1.7 miles, a quiet place to rest.

Beyond the campsite, the trail grows even steeper, often hugging the ridgeline, as

Palmer Chapel

it begins its ascent up the south flanks of Mount Sterling. As you climb, you will see some fine views of Butt Mountain to the left through the trees. The narrow pathway crosses a few small tributaries and then arrives at Good Springs Branch at 2.8 miles. There is a tumbling cascade to the left where Good Springs Branch rolls

down from Butt Mountain to spill into Palmer Creek. We turned around at this point, but you can hike on to several scenic log bridges that cross over the creek farther up the trail.

After your hike, drive a short distance up the road to visit historic Palmer Chapel, a Methodist Church built in 1898.

115

Palmer Creek Trail

Date Hiked: SPRING - May 2nd
Mileage: 6 miles Roundtrip
Our Rating: Moderate
Directions: I-40 to NC Exit 20; 0.2 mile on Route 276 to right on Cove Creek Road; follow this narrow, gravel road over mountain to intersection with paved road; turn left into Cataloochee Valley; approximately 4-5 miles to end of paved road to trail on right.

Trail Description:

Palmer Creek Trail, which actually follows Falling Rock Creek rather than Palmer Creek, was supposedly named for George Palmer, a Cataloochee set-

tler. The overall mileage for the trail includes the 1.3 miles of Pretty Hollow Gap Trail that leads to the trailhead. We had hiked Pretty Hollow Gap a week earlier, and we brought friends to share it with us this beautiful sunny spring day, a great day to get out of doors. The Pretty Hollow Gap Trail begins out of the back of the Cata-

loochee Valley where the paved road ends on the right. Follow this broad, scenic pathway for 1.3 miles to the intersection of the Palmer Creek Trail.

Palmer Creek Trail tuns left, first crossing over a long log bridge across Palmer Creek. At the bridge, Falling Rock Creek drops down from the west to tumble into Palmer Creek in a rush of waters. Falling Rock Creek has been traveling all the way down to the Cataloochee Valley from Balsam Mountain far above. The Palmer Creek Trail will follow alongside Falling Rock Creek as the pathway rises up the east flank of Balsam Mountain behind the Cataloochee Valley between the ridgelines of lower Butt Mountain to the north and Shanty Mountain to the south. After crossing the bridge, the trail begins to ascend up the right side of the creek.

Palmer Creek Trail is a narrow, single-file path, very different from the wide Pretty Hollow roadbed. It hugs the ridgeline, soon rising high above the creek. There are some moderately steep stretches as the trail rises through a lush forest. Look for large hardwood and evergreen trees missed by early loggers on this trail, like giant hemlocks 4-5 feet in diameter. Along the trailside are many natural delights including sweeps of leafy green fern, patches of soft moss,

yellow squawroot, interesting rock formations, and an assortment of wildflowers. On our spring hike we spotted trillium, daisy-like plantain, violets, bluets, buttercups, tooth-wort, and white anemone. J.L. even found a jack-in-the-pulpit nestled under the trees along the path.

At 1.1 miles after leaving Pretty Hollow Gap Trail, Palmer Creek Trail crosses Lost Bottom Creek over a foot log. The path then curls upward and around a ridge before dropping to cross Beech Creek on another foot log at 1.7 miles. Two mountain streams, Beech Creek and Falling Rock Creek, converge here in a wide, delightful setting with tumbling cascades to enjoy and broad rocks to climb on. This is a great spot for a picnic and to turn around for a 6 miles day hike— which is what we did.

Indian Flats Falls

Date Hiked: SPRING - May 9th
Mileage: 8.2 miles Roundtrip
Our Rating: Moderate
Directions: Hwy 321to Townsend Wye; right on Laurel Creek Road; first left at 0.2 mile onto Tremont Road; go 5.4 miles to end at parking area; trail starts at gate.

Trail Description:

Though this beautiful waterfall was not described in any of our hiking guides, it was marked on one of our National Geographic maps, so we decided to look for it one spring day. Having no clear directions, we might never have found it if we had not run into a hiker who had just been there! At over eight miles round trip, this hike is a longer one than the earlier hike we took on the Middle Prong Trail, but it leads to one of the prettiest falls in the Smokies and is well worth the walk.

To find Indian Flats Falls, walk up Middle Prong Trail, which rises upstream from behind the gate at the end of Tremont Road. In the first mile you pass Lynn Camp Prong Cascades on the left, a spectacular show of water pouring down stairsteps of rock layers in a bend of the creek. The trail continues up the Middle Prong and passes a junction with Panther Creek Trail at 2.3 miles. After a clearing by the creek on the left at 3 miles, the path narrows and becomes rockier. It gradually rises up above the stream into a drier woods with many hardwoods, including big-leafed Fraser magnolias. In May there is a

profusion of wildflowers.

The trail then descends from the ridge to cross Indian Flats Prong on a broad well-constructed bridge at approximately 3.7 miles. Continue following the Middle Prong Trail here as it turns to angle right up a hill after the bridge. The path curls gradually left along the side of Log Ridge, and then comes to an open area in the trail with a sharp switchback at approximately 4 miles. Stop here! The unmarked side trail to the falls at the switchback is easy to miss.

Turn right and start down the narrow trail, which winds its way through a side woods, beginning to drop sharply as it progresses. There are several steep rocky areas to climb down, but the side trail is less than a quarter mile long. The path arrives at the base of a broad, high falls tumbling more than 20 feet over a rock ledge. Below the falls is a wide pool and large, smooth rocks you can rest and picnic on. Since these spectacular falls are not well known, you may have them all to yourself. Three more levels of falls are below the first in tiers, but you may find it a scramble to get down the bank to view them. You will enjoy spending some time here before starting your journey back.

Indian Flats Falls

Chasteen Creek Trail

Date Hiked: SPRING - May 16th
Mileage: 7.2 miles Roundtrip (4 miles roundtrip to Chasteen Falls and back)
Our Rating: Moderate - Strenuous
Directions: Hwy 441 over the mountain on Newfound Gap Road to left at Smokemont Campground; follow to end of campground and trail parking.

Trail Description:

Chasteen Creek Trail is another of the trails originating out of the Smokemont area of the Smoky Mountains just before Cherokee, North Carolina. The trail curls southeasterly for 4 miles from Bradley Fork Trail to the crest of Hughes Ridge where it intersects the Hughes Ridge Trail. Rising over 1,000 feet in the first 2.5 miles, it then grows steeper, to gain another 1,500 feet or more in the last mile and a half.

To reach the trailhead of Chasteen Creek, you must first hike 1.2 miles up the Bradley Fork Trail. You will see the trail sign on the right just after crossing Chasteen Creek on a bridge. Chasteen begins on a narrower and rockier trail than Bradley Fork. At just 0.1 mile, the pathway broadens and arrives at Campsite #50 on the right. This is an open and picturesque area under the trees and a nice point for a rest on the logs.

Chasteen Creek Trail continues its uphill journey, climbing the west side of Hughes Ridge. Compared to Bradley Fork, Chasteen is a rocky, uneven

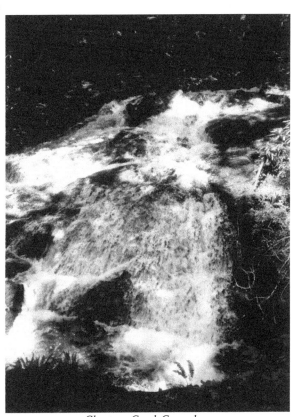

course and not as scenic. The trail gets frequent horse traffic and is very roughed up. In rainy weather it is also muddy. Although hiking guides describe the trail as following the creek, on the early portion of the hike you can only hear Chasteen Creek. However, at several points the trail drops to scenic spots by the water. One of these points to watch for is at 0.8 mile where you will see a horse stop and hitching rail on the left of the trail. A little foot path winds down behind the hitching rail to Chasteen Creek Falls, a beautiful 50-foot cascade of water tumbling over the rocks in a 15-foot drop. Since Chasteen Creek Trail is a little strenuous and difficult, for many hikers this a good turnaround point for a 4-miles roundtrip dayhike.

After the cascades, the trail climbs steeply up a ridge above the creek, where there is a good view at 1 mile, and then drops down to meet the creek again. Look for another small waterfall at 2 miles where a tributary comes downhill on the right to cross under the trail. After climbing up and over another ridge, the trail moves back down along the creekside again and arrives at Campsite #48 at 2.4 miles. This is a scenic spot between Chasteen Creek and one of its tributaries. If you have been hardy enough to make it this far before turning around you have hiked 3.6 miles overall (1.2 miles on Bradley Creek Trail and 2.4 miles

Chasteen Creek Cascades

on Chasteen Creek Trail) creating a roundtrip day hike of 7.2 miles.

Mingo Falls & Pigeon Crk.

Date Hiked: SPRING - May 23rd

Mileage: 4 miles Roundtrip (only .4 mi to the Falls and back)

Our Rating: Moderate - Strenuous

Directions: Hwy 441 over Newfound Gap and down NC side; after the Oconaluftee Visitor Center, take second left on Big Cove Road; cross Saunokee Bridge and turn left; go 4.5 miles to Mingo Campground on right; look for falls sign and parking.

Trail Description:

The path to Mingo Falls is a short, steep hike to one of the most spectacular falls in the Smoky Mountain area. This trail is not written up in any detail in any of the Smoky Mountain hiking guidebooks we could find, perhaps because it is technically on the Cherokee Indian Reservation as opposed to being inside

the National Park. However, Mingo Falls is ranked as one of the highest falls in the southeast. You should not miss it, especially since the distance to the falls and back is less than a half mile. To add to your overall hiking mileage, you can explore the nearby Pigeon Creek Trail, which starts out of the east end of Mingo Campground. You may also enjoy the Oconaluftee River Trail beside the Cherokee Visitor Center at the entrance to the National Park.

As you turn right from Big Cove Road into the campground, you will see a large sign for the Mingo Falls trailhead. The first part of the trail, which rises up a heavily walked pathway with steps built into the uphill ascent every several feet, is steep, but short. Next, a wooded trail leads around through a shaded forest to a bridge spanning Mingo Creek at the falls. You can stand on the bridge and look up in awe at the cascades falling 120 feet off a high ridge and plunging down over the rocks below. The waterfall is shaped in a long horsetail plume, narrow at the top and broadening as it shoots downward in several tiers over the rock ledges to a boulder-strewn pool. Across the bridge is a wide turnaround point in the path and a log bench. Bring your camera. You will want to take photo memories before you return to your car.

To hike another Mingo Campground trail while you are in the area, drive left approximately a mile to the end of the campground road and look for the unmarked trail to the right by the creek. This trail, known as Pigeon Creek Trail, first follows a single-file path through open woods for approximately 1.3 miles. The path ends at a stream crossing and an unmarked intersection with the Mingo Falls Trail to the right. This pathway comes out above the falls area, but the climb down to its base is treacherous and not recommended to hikers. We turned left instead to follow Pigeon Creek Trail

Awesome Mingo Falls

another half mile. High above the trail is Barnett Knob and its fire tower on the Blue Ridge Parkway. We caught a glimpse of this high 60-foot tower before turning around to head back to the campground.

123

Little Bottoms Trail

Date Hiked: SPRING - May 30th

Mileage: 7.4 miles Roundtrip

Our Rating: Strenuous

Directions: Hwy 321 from Maryville to right on Foothills Parkway; 18 miles to end of Parkway to left on Hwy 129; 0.2 mile to left into Happy Valley; turn right after 5 miles onto Abrams Creek Road and follow to Abrams ranger station parking area.

Trail Description:

To find Little Bottoms Trail, park at the Abrams Creek Ranger Station and hike about half a mile up the gravel road to the campground and through it to the gate at Cooper Road Trail. Follow Cooper Road trail another 0.9 mile to a park sign on the right at the beginning of the Little Bottoms Trail. Its name probably comes from the low bottomland along the trailside at Mill Creek.

Little Bottoms Trail has four distinct parts totaling 2.3 miles: (1) a steep, rocky, uphill section about half a mile long, (2) a similar half-mile section dropping downhill again, (3) a pleasant Abrams creekside section to Campsite #17, about 0.5 mile long, and (4) a rising and falling 0.8 mile section along the ridgeline to meet the Hatcher Mountain Trail. Little Bottoms is a rutted, uneven trail with many ups and downs around ridgelines and between stony ledges and the creekside. It narrows to only a foot wide in several places. As the mountain path climbs over many rocks and roots along its way, you must walk slowly and carefully. An old farm once lay in the bottomland, and you will marvel at how the settlers got in and out from their property on this primitive trail.

It is a demanding walk, but there are some sit-down logs and rock resting points to break the journey. The first mile, which is the most strenuous, travels southeast up over Pine Mountain and down. It is a mixed forest area with many pines. As you reach the top of Pine Mountain you can look back and see the Look Rock observation tower on Chilhowee Mountain. At 0.8 mile the trail crosses Buckshank Branch in a dip in the trail and then climbs again. At 1 mile is another stream crossing of Mill Branch, and then the trail moves into a scenc, shaded, flat section along the banks of Mill Creek. The pleasurable sights of mushrooms, flowers, ferns, and tumbling creek make it seem like a different trail. At 1.6 miles, the trail passes through Campsite #17 along the stream and, shortly after, begins to pull away from the creek to rise up and around a ridge.

After winding up and down the ridgeline, the trail ends at an intersection crossing of Hatcher Mountain Trail. Continuing on the Hatcher Mountain Trail to the right for 0.2 mile leads to an intersection with Hannah Mountain Trail on the right and a merging with the Abrams Falls Trail on the left. Another 1.7 miles on the Abrams Falls Trail will take you over a hill and down to the falls. Many hikers use this back route to get to Abrams Falls, a roundtrip hike of a little over 10 miles if you are up for a lengthier walk.

Crooked Arm Ridge Trail

Date Hiked: SPRING - June 6th
Mileage: 5.2 miles Roundtrip
Our Rating: Strenuous
Directions: Hwy 321 to Townsend Wye; right on Laurel Creek Road to end of parking lot at the beginning of Cades Cove Loop; look for trail sign on right.

Trail Description:

  This steep trail is strenuous on any day, but we chose to hike it on a windless, hot, and humid summer day. We suggest early spring, fall, or a pleasant winter day for this hike.

  To reach the trailhead, look for the Rich Mountain/Crooked Arm Trail sign on the right just as the Cades Cove Loop road begins. Follow the lowland Rich Mountain Loop Trail for 0.5 mile as the path weaves through an open forest to intersect with Crooked Arm Ridge on the right.

  The Crooked Arm Ridge Trail curls in a snakelike path for 2.1 miles in and out, up and around, the ridges to Scott Mountain. The trail begins with a gradual ascent through a shady woods with many hemlocks and pines. Soon the sounds of Crooked Arm Branch can be heard on the right below the trail. Crooked Arms Falls tumbles over the rocks at about 0.5 mile. You can scramble down the bank here on a rough side trail to get a closer look at the waterfall if you like. In wet weather the cascades spill over a rocky

126

ledge in two plumes spanning a 20 foot width before dropping 25 feet into a pool. From this point on, the Crooked Arm Ridge Trail begins to climb more steeply up a narrow pathway through mixed hardwoods. In June you will see laurel, Indian pinks, and woodland bluets along the trailside and in the fall, the colorful foliage of the oaks and maples is spectacular. This section of the trail is shady, and there are rest logs about every half mile or so, which you will welcome on the ascent. Look for views out over Cades Cove as the trail rises.

Crooked Arm climbs up and around both Crooked Ridge and Pink Ridge as it makes its way around a southern slope of Scott Mountain. It is narrow with several switchbacks as it winds in and out in a steep ascent. At three quarters of a mile, the trail angles around a ridgeline to the right and the forest opens out onto a ridgetop. You can walk to the right through an open field to an overlook for

views into the cove. You will find two more majestic views ahead at 1.2 miles and at 1.9 miles, hallmarks of this trail. After snaking left again, the pathway comes to a split at 2 miles. Either route leads a tenth of a mile to the end of the trail at an intersection. To the right the Scott Mountain Trail begins, and to the left Indian Grave Gap Trail starts its way toward Cerulean Knob.

We turned around at this junction to start the steep downhill return. For a longer hike—which we took on another cooler day—continue left on Indian Grave Gap 2.5 miles, and then take a left down Rich Mountain Loop trail for 2.9 miles more for an 8 miles roundtrip loop hike back to your car.

Kephart Prong Trail

Date Hiked: SUMMER - June 20th
Mileage: 4 miles Roundtrip
Our Rating: Moderate
Directions: Hwy 441 through Gatlinburg and up to Newfound Gap; drive down toward Cherokee 8.8 miles; trail begins on the left at pullover parking area.

Trail Description:

Kephart Prong turned out to be an unexpected treat and a delightful hike. We followed the path its full length of two miles to Kephart Shelter and the junction with Sweat Heifer Creek and Grassy Branch trails. The Kephart Prong Trail starts by crossing a large bridge, visible from the road, across the Oconaluftee River. It then turns left to wander alongside the river through a lush forest area thick with rhododendron thickets. The trail next angles right and northward up a mountain stream called the Kephart Prong, never far from the trail for the rest of its journey. The stream is a tumbling, beautiful one, with scenic footbridges at 0.3, 0.6, 1.0, and 1.4 miles. You may want to stop at all four of them—and other tempting sites—to watch the foamy cascades and the water spilling over boulders. The trail rises upward in a gradual ascent the entire way, but the pathway is wide and the climb is never too strenuous, gaining less than 850 feet overall.

Along the way, look for leafy green ferns and, in spring and summer, an assortment of wild-flowers under the trees.

There are many evidences of government and logging projects and camps to watch for as you hike. At 0.2 mile, look for the remains of an old Civilian Conservation Corps (CCC) camp. There are traces of rock hearths and walls, a stone fountain, a chimney, and a section of boxwoods where the buildings and barracks of the camp used to be. Shortly after the first bridge crossing over Kephart Prong, at approximately one half mile on the left, you may see the foundation remains of an old fish hatchery, too, built and run by the government Works Project Administration. At the second bridge crossing, take a break to enjoy the cascades here. Farther on, at about 0.8 mile, watch for remnants of the old logging railroad that used to pass through this area. After two more crossings of the stream, the path opens and comes to a trail junction and an open clearing with a covered shelter and a big fireplace by the stream. This is a nice picnic spot. Sweat Heifer Creek Trail branches left out of the junction here, and Grassy Branch Trail leads on up Richland Mountain behind the shelter to Dry Sluice Gap. Kephart Prong Trail, the stream, shelter, and Mount Kephart above on the Appalachian Trail are all named in honor of Horace Kephart, who helped establish the national park in the Smokies.

Brushy Mountain Trail

Date Hiked: SUMMER - July 4th

Mileage: 6.4 miles Roundtrip

Our Rating: Strenuous

Directions: Hwy 441 into Gatlinburg; left on Hwy 321 at Traffic Light #3; drive approximately 6 miles to right on Greenbrier Road; drive approximately 4 miles to trailhead and parking at end of road.

Trail Description:

The first mile leading to Brushy Mountain Trail follows Porters Creek Trail out of the end of Greenbrier Road. The hike on Porters Creek Trail is an easy walk on an old settlers' road along the creek. At 1 mile up Porters Creek, the trail splits at an open intersection called Porters Flats. Instead of continuing left along the stream on the Porters Creek Trail, take the path that angles right, where you will see a trail marker for Brushy Mountain Trail. The trailway weaves into the woods, heading west toward Gatlinburg.

This is a quiet woods trail, sometimes narrow and rocky, winding up the eastern ridges of Brushy Mountain. It runs to the left of the historic John Messer farm in the first quarter mile. You can see the farm site through the trees, and a side-trail leads over to the restored log house, barn, and springhouse. The Brushy Mountain Trail also crosses two shallow creeks in the early section, and there are frequent evidences of old homesites, particularly rock walls. Although you often hear the Long Branch stream to the right of the path, Brushy Mountain Trail never drops down close to it or alongside it. At about 0.7 mile, the trail

rises to an open area high above the stream where you can see this mountain stream crashing through the valley below. After this scenic point, the trail switches back sharply left to curl up the mountain ridgeline.

Brushy Mountain Trail is mostly an uphill trudge, gradual at first but becoming steeper as the trail climbs. It gains 1,275 feet in the first two miles and over 2,500 feet before reaching Trillium Gap on the summit of Brushy Mountain. There are some breaks in the ascent when the trail winds down at several points to cross small creeks and shallow rills before rising up again. These are pretty spots and places to stop for a minute and explore. You may find a salamander under a creek rock or see gray squirrels chattering in the treetops.

The trail is probably named for the dense, brushy thickets of mountain laurel, rhododendron, and other shrubs that cover much of Brushy Mountain. Even on the lower portion of the trail you will see thick stands of laurel and rhododendron. The area has an interesting diversity of trees. Look for big magnolias with huge leaves in the lower forest, hemlocks mixed with many hardwoods as the trail rises, and silver bells, beeches, and pines farther up. We also saw many varieties of mushrooms and summer wildflowers on our July hike. At 2.2 miles there is a big rock in the middle of the path, and there are fine views at this open point of both Brushy Mountain and Mount Le Conte. This is a good place to stop for lunch and to turn around for a 6.4 miles overall roundtrip hike.

Mingus Mill Creek Trail

Date Hiked: SUMMER - July 18th

Mileage: 5 miles Roundtrip

Our Rating: Moderate

Directions: Hwy 441 through Gatlinburg and on to Newfound Gap; continue past Smokemont Campground approximately 3 miles, the Mingus Mill sign is on the right.

Trail Description:

Maps are not in unity about this trail's name. Since there is no trail sign, we labeled it Mingus Mill Creek Trail to match the name on Earthwalk Press's hiking guide and map. This name also distinguishes it from Mingus

Creek Trail, which rises out of the Cooper Creek area at Deeplow Gap. The parking area for this trailhead is at Mingus Mill, a working turbine grain mill that the park service runs and maintains. It is a treat to see this mill as part of your hike, and signs direct you from the parking area to the millhouse. An early waterwheel mill was built on this site in the 1700s, later replaced by the existing three-storied turbine mill in the 1800s. You can go into the lower floor of the building to learn how grain was milled and watch the

water powered turbine churn corn into cornmeal. After exploring the mill, you can stroll up a nature trail that takes you by the high millrace and then alongside the lower wooden flume that brings water from the dam down to the mill.

The Mingus Creek trailhead begins

behind the gate at the end of the parking lot. You can see the mill and the beginning of the millrace, flume, and dam to the left as you start your hike. The first section of the trail is an open roadbed wandering along the right side of Mingus Creek. This enjoyable shady woods trail ascends gradually along the stream, crisscrossing it several times on nice footbridges. We saw many varieties of colorful mushrooms on this trail in July.

At 0.5 mile is a target range and picnic tables and at 1 mile is a water treatment supply plant for Oconaluftee. A footlog bridge takes you across Madcap Branch where it tumbles into Mingus Creek. This stream crossing is a scenic point. After the bridge, the pathway narrows and climbs upward, rising above the creek. It passes a small cemetery, and at about 2.4 miles the trail rises to a rocky, exposed summit. There are big boulders here to sit on and a sign pointing toward another cemetery side-trail to the right. The path then descends through a rougher, grassy, and less maintained area to come to a rotted and broken down footlog that crosses high over a deep, swift section of the Mingus Creek. The crumbling log bridge was too dangerous to walk over. We explored but could find no other route from one high bank to the other, so we turned around to start back at this point. The continuing trail would lead approximately a half-mile further to end at an intersection with the Mingus Creek Trail.

Jakes Creek Trail

Date Hiked: SUMMER - August 29th
Mileage: 6.6 miles Roundtrip
Our Rating: Strenuous
Directions: Hwy 441 through Gatlinburg to Sugarlands Visitor Center; right on Little River Road to left into Elkmont at sign; 1.5 miles to trail signs just before campground entrance and turn left at signs; drive 1 mile to end of road and parking area for trailhead.
Trail Description:

      The Jakes Creek Trail climbs out of the Elkmont area heading toward trails that link to the Appalachian Trail high above. The unrelieving march gains approximately 2,000 feet from the parking area to Jakes Gap at 4,055 feet at the trail's end. The trailhead begins behind a gate at the back of the parking area and then begins to follow an old railroad bed that gradually narrows as it ascends. At 0.3 mile the road passes the sign for Cucumber Gap Trail to the left and at 0.4 mile the trailhead for Meigs Mountain Trail to the right. Jakes continues always straight ahead.

      Although steep, the hike is scenic and pleasant. You can soon hear Jakes Creek tumbling to the right. Before the first mile ends, the trail moves closer to the creekside, and you will see the stream cascade over the rocks below. Shortly afterwards, a short path leads down to a waterfall and a deep swimming pool on the right. This is a great spot for a rest and a good place to cool your feet on a hot day. Farther up Jakes Creek, the trail rockhops across Waterdog Branch at

another pleasing spot. Look for twining grape-vines, white quartz, and large Fraser magnolias all along this trail. Many rhododendron grow alongside the trail and the streamsides, dark green and shiny and often thick with white and pink blooms in early to mid July.

After the first bridge crossing, Jakes Creek Trail grows steeper and narrower, rising up a ridge and then down again before traveling over another stream, the Newt Prong. It then climbs upward on the ridgelines of Blanket Mountain and drops down to a final crossing over Jakes Creek at approximately 2 miles. The trail switches back left after this point, now traveling along the right side of the creek for about one half mile farther until it comes to Campsite #27 on the left at 2.5 miles. Here you

can enjoy a rest and perhaps a backpack lunch under the trees by Jakes Creek, which has become much narrower and more shallow. As the trail continues, the creek will simply disappear as it reaches its source.

After the campsite, the Jakes Creek Trail climbs more steeply for another 0.8 mile to finally arrive at Jakes Gap between Blanket Mountain and Dripping Spring Mountain. Here the pathway ends at an intersection with the Miry Ridge and Pan-ther Creek trails, 3.3 miles from the start of the trail.

Scott Mountain Trail

Date Hiked: SUMMER - September 17th
Mileage: 9 miles Roundtrip
Our Rating: Moderate
Directions: Hwy 321 to Townsend Wye; right on Laurel Creek Road for 3.9 miles to Schoolhouse Gap trail parking area on the right side of the road.

Trail Description:

To get to Scott Mountain trailhead, you must hike 2.2 miles on Schoolhouse Gap Trail, a frequently hiked roadbed trail rising southwest up Spence Branch to Dorsey Gap and then up the east ridge of Scott Mountain to dead end at an intersection with the Scott Mountain Trail. The ascent on the Schoolhouse Gap Trail is gradual. You will know you are nearing the beginning of Scott Mountain Trail when Schoolhouse Gap begins to run alongside the park boundary and by a mountain residence with a picnic table behind it on the right side of the trail. Scott Mountain Trail angles to the left up the slope of Scott Mountain at this point. Unlike the wide and rocky roadbed of Schoolhouse Gap Trail, Scott Mountain Trail is a single-file path. Beautiful in the fall, it is soft underfoot and not heavily traveled by hikers.

The first half-mile of the trail winds steeply up the side of Scott Mountain following the park boundary. In places the trail is very narrow and slanted, hugging the ridgeline and looking down on the left to deep sinkhole areas and valleys known for their limestone caves. One well-known cavern is the Blowhole cave, and the area between Dorsey Gap and Scott Mountain, laced with limestone dips and depressions, is called the Whiteoak Sink. You will find a

description of the Whiteoak Sink Trail later in this book on pp. 226-227.

Scott Mountain continues its climb to a ridge top high above the Whiteoak Sink in approximately a half mile and then curls around and walks along the mountain top for a short time. This area of the trail is delightful with fine views to either side for about a half-mile. The path

passes through pine woods here with a thick bed of pine needles under your feet, quiet and peaceful except for the rustling of the breeze in the pine trees. Many varieties of moss and fern grow along the trail. After crossing the ridge, the trail begins to drop downwhill At about 1.8 miles, the trail reaches a small gap, where the path crosses over a shallow tributary on the rocks. Look for a giant 50-inch diameter tulip tree on the left side of the trail here. If you hike on, you may see many large trees that missed the axes of the early loggers, especially tulip poplars and silverbells. After the gap, Scott Mountain Trail rises again, often switching in and out as it climbs another ridgeline. The trail is steep and narrow in this section and somewhat eroded, so watch your footing. We turned around at 2.3 miles after passing two giant silverbell trees.

Look Rock Trail

Date Hiked: FALL - October 8th
Mileage: 1 mile only Roundtrip
Our Rating: Moderate
Directions: Hwy 321 from Maryville to Foothills Parkway on the right; drive 11 miles to Look Rock sign; parking lot is on left after the sign and start of the trail.

Trail Description:

A journey over the Foothills Parkway is an 18-mile scenic drive at any season, but especially beautiful in the fall months when the foliage is at peak. Visitors can take the short walk up to the Look Rock observation tower while in the area to see incredible views out over the mountain ranges. This short trail is easy to hike with grandparents, children, or visitors. Friends joined us this day, and we drove on over to Abrams Campground with them to picnic and walk up a section of the Cooper Road Trail. You could also picnic in the Foothills Campground area near the Look Rock Trail and walk along the quiet paved roads that weave through the wooded campground.

To begin this trail, park at the lot on the left just after the Look Rock and

Foothills Campground signs. Walk back up the road on the sidewalk until you see the trail sign across the street. The well-travelled walkway begins there, starting south and then turning west to climb up the high ridgetop to the tower. Only half a mile long, the path is steep, but there are several rest spots along the way. The trail wanders up through an

open woods, pretty and strewn with russet, yellow, and orange leaves in the fall. At 0.2 mile, the trail curves left and soon passes by a fenced park monitoring station on the right. There is a fine view from the rocks behind the station that you might want to walk over to see.

Continuing up the trail, you will soon reach the Look Rock park tower ahead of you. Climb up the tower to the railed observatory area. Signs there tell you the names of the mountain ranges you can see in all directions as you walk around the tower. There are stunning panoramic views toward the Smokies to Rich Mountain and the Cades Cove hills and on beyond to the high Smokies ranges of Mount Le Conte, Thunderhead Mountain, Cove Mountain, and Mount Guyot. To the north are scenic vistas of the foothills and mountain ranges toward Maryville, Knoxville, and beyond. On a clear day the views are especially stunning, so bring your binoculars.

Even in the heaviest tourist seasons in the Smokies, the Foothills Parkway is seldom crowded. You will not find the slow bumper-to-bumper traffic as in many areas of the mountains, and the show of fall colors is often more spectacular than farther up in the mountains. Plan to drive the full length of the parkway while you are here and stop to enjoy the vistas at the many pullovers along the road.

Mountain views from atop Look Rock Tower   139

Bullhead Trail

Date Hiked: FALL - October 15th
Mileage: 7.4 miles Roundtrip
Our Rating: Strenuous
Directions: Hwy 441 into Gatlinburg; left on Airport Road at Traffic Light #8; continue onto Cherokee Orchard Road and to trailhead just before the beginning of one-way Roaring Fork Motor Nature Trail; park at Rainbow Falls parking area on right.
Trail Description:

Bullhead Mountain is one of the lower mountains below the slopes of Mount Le Conte. The Bullhead Trail provides a main pathway to Mount Le Conte and the Le Conte Lodge and is the trail used to take supplies up to the lodge by llamas. You might see these interesting pack animals coming or going on your hike. Know in advance that this trail is a strenuous, steep one for whatever mileage you wish to hike and that the return trip is as hard on tired calves, knees, and feet as the uphill climb.

To hike the Bullhead Trail, follow the pathway from the parking lot to the sign for the Rainbow Falls Trail on the left. Continue right past the sign down a short path that leads to a gravel roadbed. Turn left on the roadbed, which is actually the end of the Old Sugarlands Trail. After 0.7 mile from the parking lot, turn left at the trail sign onto Bullhead Trail.

The trail starts through the woods and begins to rise quickly. The forest here has a variety of hardwoods, colorful in the fall, mixed with hemlocks, laurel, and rhododendron. In the first half mile up the trail, you will gain 500 feet in elevation and begin to see peaks of the valley and mountains to your left as you

climb. Watch your footing, as the pathway has frequent tree roots to cross and many rocky areas. At approximately 1 mile, the path turns and moves through an open section between large cliff formations and giant boulders. This area looks like a rock quarry. Huge rocks rise high up the hillside and then down to a low dip alongside the trail. After this point, the trail curls around to the right to begin climbing steeply up a ridgeline of Bullhead Mountain. As the trail rises and angles left, you will see views of the valley to the right from several open points along the trailside.

At a particularly large boulder by the side of the path at 1.5 to 2 miles, you will enjoy an exceptional vista across Sugarland Mountain, Blanket Mountain, and beyond. In the spring, hikers can spot wildflowers among the rocky outcroppings along the trail, including hepatica, trillium, trailing arbutus and violets, and in the fall the colorful foliage is spectacular. Small balds appear farther up Bullhead, and you can see these open spaces, often covered in heath. The peak of Bullhead Mountain is now above you and resembles a bull when viewed from a distance, giving the mountian and the trail its name. As you

continue climbing, the trail switches in and out around the Bullhead, opening out again and again to fine panoramic views. We hiked three miles on the trail to the rock pulpit and overlook built by the CCC (Civilian Conservation Corps). Two or more can sit at this overlook for lunch with a view to die for.

141

Juney Whank Falls

Date Hiked: FALL - October 22nd
Mileage: 1 mile Roundtrip
Our Rating: Moderate
Directions: Hwy 441 over Newfound Gap to Cherokee, NC; right on Hwy 19; right on Everett to cross the river into Bryson City; follow the signs three miles to Deep Creek Campground.

Trail Description:

Deep Creek is a beautiful campground hidden away on what many hikers term the backside of the Smokies. Clear road signs lead from Bryson City to the campground area. After entering the campground, drive through the picnic area to the rear to park. You will first see signage for the Deep Creek and Indian Creek trails, soon followed by the park sign to Juney Whank Falls approximately 400 yards farther on the right. Because Juney Whank is so short, we hiked Indian Creek Trail (page 144) on the same day.

The hike to Juney Whank Falls is relatively steep but less than a half mile to the falls (0.3 mile to the falls; 0.6 mile roundtrip just to falls and back). After a short distance into the woods, the trail splits. There is no marker to direct you at this point, but stay right to continue on to the falls. The trail winds upward through the woods, soon curling around a ridgeline, twining in and out a few times as it climbs. A steep ravine falls off to the right, and the path is somewhat

narrow. After curling around the ravine, the trail angles left up through a thicker wooded area. As the trail continues climbing, it soon follows high along the left side of noisy Deep Creek. After the trail begins to drop, you will hear the sound of the falls ahead.

The Juney Whank Branch tumbles in from the left at 0.3 mile to meet Deep Creek in a long spill of water. Juney Whank Falls is actually more of a cascade than a waterfall, as the water rolls down and over a series of rocky ledges for over 90 feet. A path drops down from the main trail to cross a footlog bridge at the falls. The path is a little steep, and very muddy in wet weather, so watch your footing as you descend toward the falls. The footbridge crosses directly over the chute in the middle of the falls. You can look upstream from the bridge to see the upper 40 feet of water coming over the rocks toward you, and then look downstream from the bridge to see the lower 50 feet of the cascades spilling down into Deep Creek. It's a pretty place, and the sound of falling water fills your ears. There are rocks to sit on at the bridge. An ongoing path continues after the falls, which you can walk along for a while, but it soon branches off in numerous directions with no trail guides or markers. Juney Whank continues 1.2 miles further to intersect the Deep Creek Trail but without a clear trail sign, it is hard to know which pathway to follow. We explored approximately 0.2 mile beyond the falls but then turned around to start our return.

Juney Whank Falls

143

Indian Creek Trail

Date Hiked: FALL - October 22nd
Mileage: 5.8 miles Roundtrip
Our Rating: Moderate
Directions: Hwy 441 over Newfound Gap to Cherokee, NC; right on Hwy 19; right on Everett to cross the river into Bryson City; follow the signs three miles to Deep Creek Campground.

Trail Description:

Indian Creek Trail starts at the back end of the Deep Creek Campground. The open roadbed trail is a nice walk even for beginning hikers. We explored this trail the same fall day we hiked to nearby Juney Whank Falls (page 142), which was only a short roundtrip walk.

You will see both the Deep Creek and Indian Creek trail names on the trailhead sign. The first 0.7 mile follows the Deep Creek Trail, which rises gradually through an open woods of hardwoods and hemlocks. Deep Creek, a scenic lowland stream here, wanders along to the right of the trailside. At 0.2 mile, watch for a log bench on the right and picturesque Tom Branch Falls tumbling 50 feet over rocky ledges down the opposite hillside. After the falls, the trail continues on to a bridge crossing at 0.5 mile, and then begins to climb a little more steeply. The pathway arrives at a fork in the road at 0.7 mile where Deep Creek and Indian Creek intersect. Turn right at this intersection to start up the Indian Creek Trail.

Indian Creek Falls

Like the Deep Creek trail, the Indian Creek Trail follows the route of an old settlers' road, winding in a gradual uphill journey along the banks of a valley stream between Thomas and Sunkota ridges. The fall colors of October were glorious on our hike. At approximately 200 feet from the start of the trail, behind a log bench on the left, you will see a side path that leads down to Indian Creek Falls. Larger than Tom Branch, this waterfall plunges 60 feet over a drop in the stream to a big pool below. It's a good spot to rest and take photos.

As you continue along the main trail, the pathway next crosses Indian Creek over a log bridge to travel along the left side of the stream. At 0.5 mile from the beginning of Indian Creek Trail a sign marks the beginning of Stone Pile Gap Trail, which winds downhill to the right to cross Indian Creek on a footlog. Shortly after this intersection at 0.8 mile, a loop trail branches left to climb steeply up over Sunkota Ridge and down to intersect the Deep Creek Trail on the other side. If you want to hike the loop, the overall round trip is approximately 7 miles, but continuing up Indian Creek is the easier choice. The trail journeys on, curling gently up the valley with only a gradual ascent. The path rises away from the creek into the forest for a while but later returns. At 1.5 miles from the start of the trailhead a little cemetery lies off to the left, and then, in a section along the stream again, there are many scenic pools and cascades. We stopped for lunch by the streamside and turned around at a wide wooden bridge over Indian Creek at 2.2 miles from the start of the trail and 2.9 miles from the start of our hike.

Tapoco Trail

Date Hiked: FALL - November 14th
Mileage: 6 miles Roundtrip
Our Rating: Strenuous
Directions: Hwy 321 to right on Foothills Parkway; left at end of Parkway on Hwy 129 over the mountain to Deals Gap; after the Gap, stay to the right on Hwy 129 where Hwy 28 to Fontana intersects; the road drops down to cross the bridge below the Cheoah Dam; trail parking is just across the dam on the right.

Trail Description:

Tapoco Trail is not actually in the Great Smoky Mountains National Park proper but is about 2.5 miles outside its boundary at the edge of the Joyce Kilmer

Slickrock Wilderness near the Twentymile area. Immediately after crossing the bridge below Cheoah Dam, turn into the gravel parking lot to the right. There is no trail sign here, but you will find one on the left as you start up the pathway. The trail winds along the ridgeline above Calderwood Lake, turning back southward to climb along Slickrock Creek to Lower Falls.

The early part of the trail, branching west from the parking lot, is wide and in November was strewn with a colorful carpet of yellow and orange maple leaves. From the start, the path is seldom out of sight of beautiful Calderwood Lake on the right. By 1 mile, the trail has risen high above the lake and become very narrow. Not a good hiking choice for those who
146

are troubled by heights, the trail coils along the ridgeline with steep drops to the right. The pathway is sometimes a little treacherous as you clamber over rocks and roots along a thin trail hanging above the lake. In a few areas, the soil is actually falling away, so watch your footing carefully. There are four high, narrow bridges to cross, skirting over small tributaries or around rocky ledges. When we hiked, many of the bridges had loose boards (scary) and needed to be navigated with caution.

At approximately 1.5 miles, the trail begins to angle left up a cove in the lake. At the back of the cove, Slickrock Creek spills down into Calderwood Lake. From this point on, Tapoco Trail changes character dramatically, becoming a more typical mountain trail instead of a lakeside walk, as it begins its journey up a side ridge of the Unicoi Mountains along the creek. The trail winds in a crooked route along the left side of the creekbank, climbing steadily, and sometimes steeply, while working its way over rocks and tree roots. This area of the Tapoco Trail is known for its wildflowers in the spring and is called the Hanging Gardens. There are pretty scenes here all along the stream and, at approximately 3 miles, there is a series of cascades and falls called Slickrock or Lower Falls. Below the falls is a good hiking destination and a fine place for a picnic lunch.

After your hike, drive up the road to check out the Historic Tapoco Lodge on the banks of the Cheoah River, a nice place to stay if you have the time.

147

Beard Cane Trail

Date Hiked: WINTER - January 1st
Mileage: 10 miles Roundtrip
Our Rating: Strenuous
Directions: Hwy 321 from Maryville to right on Foothills Parkway; drive 9 miles to left on Flats Road; stay right at campground entrance and follow Flats Road left into Top of the World Community at sign; at 2 miles turn right on Jouroulman Drive into Park Lane Heights; take first right on Steffner Circle; unmarked trailhead on right of road at 0.1 mile; park on left in pullover.

Trail Description:

We hiked in to Beard Cane Trail on a mild winter day in January. This is not a short hike, as it is 2.7 miles just to get to the trailhead of Beard Cane and

not an easy 2.7 miles of hiking. The first mile, which follows the Gold Mine Trail, is rocky and difficult to walk. Gold Mine Trail climbs down from Steffner Road in the Top of the World subdivision on a rutty, rough roadbed into the Park to intersect the Cooper Road Trail at Gold Mine Gap. Stop for a rest here on the logs before heading left on Cooper Road.

The Cooper Road Trail, which has traveled from Abrams Campground to the gap for nearly three miles, now begins to drop through the woods on its wide roadbed. At 0.5 mile from the intersection with the Gold Mine Trail, it arrives at Cane Gap, where the Cane Gap trailhead drops off to the left. Cooper Road angles on to the right to begin a climb of 1.7 miles up to a saddle gap at the junction of Hatcher Mountain Trail and Beard Cane Trail. This middle portion of the 11 miles long Cooper Road, which connects Abrams Campground to Cades Cove, is mostly uphill and it has some steep, rocky sections along the way. We enjoyed the winter landscape and the shapes of the tree branches against a blue sky. At a switchback at a high point on Hatcher Mountain you can look back northeast toward the

Chilhowee Mountains to see Look Rock on the Foothills Parkway. Along this crest, the trail flattens out for a space of relief before rolling down and around the ridge and then up again to finally arrive at the junction of Hatcher Mountain Trail on the right. The intersection of Beard Cane follows on the left less than a quarter mile later.

Unlike the wide Cooper Road, Beard Cane Trail is a narrow, single-file path, 4.2 miles in total length, with a soft footing, strewn with pine needles. After the first quarter mile, the trail begins to drop, curling gradually downhill between Hatcher and Beard Cane mountains to arrive in a low hollow along Beard Cane Creek. The creek on the right of the path is narrow at first but soon increases in size as it tumbles down through the valley. At approximately 1 mile from the start of Beard Cane Trail the shaded pathway arrives at Beard Cane Campsite #11. This is a nice camping or picnic area under the trees with the stream right nearby. From this point on, the trail is pleasantly flat. It winds through the valley along the creek, rock-hopping back and forth over the water. We walked another 1.3 miles beyond the campsite before turning back, for an overall roundtrip hike of 10 miles.

Chimney Tops Trail

Date Hiked: WINTER - February 6th
Mileage: 4 miles Roundtrip
Our Rating: Strenuous
Directions: Hwy 441 through Gatlinburg and up the mountain past Sugarlands Visitor Center; the Chimneys parking area is 6+ miles up on the right.
Trail Description:

Some hikes in the Smokies are short-but-sweet, but the Chimney Tops Trail would be better described as short, steep, and tough. We had hiked so many more idyllic trails before this one, that we were amazed at the popularity of this spot. From the trail's reputation, I guess we expected something more remarkable. The parking area is always packed and the pathway always heavily peopled. One of the park rangers told us this is due to the trail's high visibility on the main highway over the Smoky Mountains and the thrill aspect of hiking to the towering Chimney Top rocks.

The trail begins pleasantly through the woods, crossing three bridges over Walker Camp Prong and Road Prong in the first 0.3 mile. The streams are scenic with large boulders and rushing cascades, the banks lined with lush, green rhododendron. The narrowing pathway then switches left, and the climb begins, as the trail starts curling up the side of Sugarland Mountain. At 0.8 mile another footbridge crosses the Road Prong, and at 0.9 mile the trail meets the intersection of the

Road Prong Trail on the left before widening into a broad open area known as Beech Flats. Here Chimney Tops Trail turns right, leaving the streams behind, and beginning to climb sharply upward toward the rocky mountain peaks above.

   The trail narrows now, becoming a dirt pathway, rough and rocky underfoot and well worn-down from throngs of tourists. It winds upward, swinging gradually left and then switching back sharply right around a ridge point at approximately 1.5 miles. We had additional difficulty hiking this section of the trail after a very rainy season in the Smokies. The path was muddy and slick, with long sections of deep muddy bogs that sucked at our boots and slowed our ascent. In the last mile, the trail grows steeper and steeper until it arrives at the rocky promontory base of the Chimneys and a warning sign to "Stop Here." There are huge boulders at the trail's end to picnic on and fine views off the mountain top.

Views from the top on Chimney Tops

   If sure of foot and not afraid of heights, hikers can follow the narrow side trail around the boulders to get to the base of the chimneys and can climb up the rock ledges, using well-worn toe-holds, to attain the summit of the Chimney Tops. From here the adventurous can walk carefully out to sit high on the Chimney Top rocks and look in all directions at the wonderful views. You can see the Newfound Gap Road below, and the ranges of Mount Le Conte, the Bullhead, Mount Mingus, and Sugarland Mountain.

151

Low Gap Trail

Date Hiked: WINTER - February 19th
Mileage: 6.6 miles Roundtrip
Our Rating: Strenuous
Directions: I-40E to Exit 443 at Foothills Parkway; follow Parkway onto Hwy 321/32, staying on Hwy 32 to road to Cosby Campground; drive 3 miles to end of campground and trail parking.

Trail Description:

Low Gap is a connector trail that runs approximately 2.9 miles from the Cosby Creek valley to meet the Appalachian Trail high above. The steep trail gains over 1,750 feet of elevation as it follows near Cosby Creek through a lush, deep forest.

The trailhead starts at the back of the Cosby Campground after a short walk from the hiker parking area. The initial 0.4 mile uphill hike, along campground roads from the hiker parking area to the trailhead adds 0.8 mile to the overall round-trip hiking distance. In winter, usually between October to April, the Cosby Campground is closed off to campers and vehicles but the area is open

to hikers. Walk behind the gate and follow the paved road veering to the left where it splits. Look for the trail sign on the left of the road as it curls around in a loop.

Low Gap is a roadbed trail for the first 0.3 mile, climbing steadily up the northwest side of the Mount Cammerer ridges between Rocky Face Mountain and Camel Hump Mountain. A horse trail comes in to the right at 0.2 mile, and the roadbed trail ends in a loop turnaround. The Low Gap Trail continues on through two large boulders at the back of this loop, now becoming a more narrow pathway. The trail here is soft underfoot and pleasant, winding upward through an open woods. There are many pine and hemlock trees, with fern and moss by the sides of the path. At a footlog crossing about 0.4 mile up the trail, a small waterfall cascades

down between moss-covered boulders. This is a pretty point along the hike. Shortly after this bridge, an unmarked side trail angles left, leading down to the Mount Cammerer Trail and back over to the campground.

Where the early section of the trail traversed mostly at a distance from Cosby Creek, the trail now begins to parallel the creek for over a half mile. There is another beautiful cascades worth watching for at 1.2 miles before the trail switches back left and up into a deeper forest of hemlock and hardwoods. Watch for many giant trees, tall and broad, in this forest section where the lumber was not logged prior to establishment of the park. At 1.8 miles is an odd boulder field to the left of the trail. As Low Gap continues, the pathway grows increasingly steep. The climb is rather unrelenting once the trail moves away from the creek, but the forest is deep and lush with overhanging trees, fern, moss, and rhododendron along the way. We lunched where Low Gap met the last of Cosby Creek again at approximately 2.5 miles. Beyond the creek, the trail follows a side ridge for another 0.4 mile to meet a crossing of the Appalachian Trail at Low Gap. Turning around at this point creates a 6.6 miles roundtrip journey. From the Appalachian Trail, Low Gap continures on winding its way downhill for 2.5 miles to meet the Big Creek Trail on the other side of the mountain at Walnut Bottom.

Snake Den Ridge Trail

Date Hiked: WINTER - February 25th
Mileage: 5 miles Roundtrip
Our Rating: Strenuous
Directions: I-40E to Exit 443 at Foothills Parkway; follow Parkway into Hwy 321/32, staying on Hwy 32 to road to Cosby Campground; follow road 3 miles to end and hiker parking.

Trail Description:

      Snake Den Ridge Trail winds uphill, in a continuous ascent between Snake Den Mountain and Inadu Mountain for 5.3 miles, gaining over 3,000 feet in elevation before reaching its terminus with the Appalachian Trail on Inadu Knob. Inadu is a Cherokee word for "snake," and there may be snakes in this area since the trail hugs a south-facing ridgeline, a locale snakes favor. Records do show an early settler, Joseph Campbell, discovered a den of rattlesnakes in this area—probably giving the mountain, ridge, and trail their names. We did not see any on our hike in February and most hiking guides do not report spotting snakes on this trail.

      Like Low Gap Trail, this trail also begins from the back of the Cosby Campground area. Across from the amphitheater, and beyond the gate, follow the paved road between campsites B1 and B2 for a half mile to the trail marker on the right by campsite B51. The first section of the hike is uphill on a gravel roadbed. At 0.3 mile is a junction where a Cosby horse trail leads left to connect with Low Gap Trail. Snake Den Ridge Trail continues right, becoming softer underfoot and weaving through a pleasant woods. The way is steep, but there

are interesting remnants of community life along the way. An old wall runs to the left after a culvert crossing and a well-kept cemetery sits on the right at 0.5 mile in a grassy clearing. Here are buried many Campbells, Williamsons, and the Poet Laureate of the Smokies, Ella Costner, whose grave you should look for. At 0.8 mile, the trail comes to a loop turn. At the back of the loop, the trail continues between two boulders. To the right of the clearing, you can walk out on a concrete slab and look far below to see Rock Creek tumbling down the valley.

The trail narrows now, becoming a deep forest path and a pretty place to hike, even in winter. There are many lush ferns and mosses here among large hemlock and hardwood trees. At approximately 1.1 miles, Snake Den arrives at a scenic crossing of Rock Creek, where a log footbridge straddles the rushing creek with foamy cascades plunging between moss-covered boulders. The trail continues upward after Rock Creek and begins to make snake-like switches and turns as it rises. There are many rhododendron here. At 2 miles, Snake Den drops to a crossing of Inadu Creek. Here, as at Rock Creek, there are lovely waterfalls near the stream crossing but no bridge at this stream, making this crossing difficult with high water. For a 5-mile (2 miles + 0.5 mile to trailhead doubled) roundtrip hike, this is a good spot to picnic and rest before starting back down the trail. Continuing on, the path narrows, growing rockier and steeper and passing through scraggly heath stands, before

reaching the Maddron Bald junction at 4.6 miles and the trail's end at 5.3 miles.

Cataloochee Divide Trail

Date Hiked: WINTER - March 3rd
Mileage: 7 miles Roundtrip
Our Rating: Moderate
Directions: I-40E to NC Exit 20; 0.2 mile to right on Cove Creek Road; approximately 5.8 miles on this gravel road to Cove Creek Gap at top of mountain; trail on right with pullover parking.
Trail Description:

Early spring is an excellent time to explore trails crossing high ridge tops in the Smokies because the trees are not fully leafed out and the views are more spectacular. Cataloochee Divide Trail straddles the top of Cataloochee Mountain

with panoramas northwest into Cataloochee Valley and beyond to the Smoky Mountain ranges and with fine vistas southeast across the North Carolina valleys to Pisgah and Balsam mountains. The trailhead begins at Cove Creek Gap at a high point on the Catalochee Mountain. There is a pullover parking area for several vehicles at the top of the hill.

Cataloochee Divide swings left from the road and travels southwest, following the park boundary along the top of the divide for most all of its journey.

The trail begins with a gradual ascent from the road up the ridge through a mixed forest. The footing is loamy and soft, not rocky, and easy to walk on. The trail, generally, is undulating with level sections tucked in between the rolling ascents and descents. This is a good trail

for beginning hikers or families with children. The pace and footing are not difficult, and there are many interesting things to see along the journey.

Look for pinecones, hickory nuts, acorns, many varieties of trees, and laurel and rhododendron in the first mile. You will soon see the first of many park boundary fence lines to the left of the trail built by the CCC in the 1930s. Early March is too soon for most wild flowers, but you may notice the leaves and buds of many future spring flowers, like violets or wood lilies along the pathway, or sight deer. After the first mile, the trail levels off for approximately a half mile and offers the first glimpses of the Cataloochee Valley to the right and soon more views out across the fence lines to the left. At 1.5 miles is an open clearing, a rest log, and spectacular Cataloochee Valley and Smokies vistas.

The trail then drops, and at 2 miles is a broad grassy clearing with a picture-perfect scene to Cove Creek Valley below. Farther on, an old farm road angles downhill to the left of the trail toward private lands below. This area is known as Panther Spring Gap, a saddle gap between the national park and the Suttontown area of North Carolina. After the gap, the trail climbs again for about a mile before leveling and returning at 3 miles to the boundary fence line and a large field. There are more scenic overlooks at this point and in the next half mile. We lunched and turned around at 3.5 miles at a covered bench just off the trailside called Taylor's Turnaround. A worn sign marks the spot, and this open area, with its views out over the Cataloochee Valley makes a good turnaround point for a 7 miles roundtrip hike. To hike further, Cataloochee Divide meets McKee Branch Trail at 4.6 miles and ends, after climbing to Double Gap at 4,600 feet at an intersection with Hemphill Bald Trail.

Oconaluftee River Trail

Date Hiked: WINTER - March 12th
Mileage: 3 miles Roundtrip
Our Rating: Easy
Directions: Hwy 441 through Gatlinburg and up over Newfound Gap and down mountain to the Oconaluftee Visitor Center before Cherokee, NC.
Trail Description:

The Oconaluftee River Trail starts behind the Visitor's Center in Cherokee, turning to the right just before the fencing that surrounds the Mountain Farm Museum. This is a short, easy trail, and there is time before or after the hike to walk through the farm museum of the early 1900s. This is a collection of buildings moved here by the park to create an authentic pioneer farm community. There are log houses, barns, and outbuildings with a nice trail weaving through the fenced farm community.

The 1.5 miles Oconaluftee Trail first strolls alongside the farm fence and then curls left to follow the Oconaluftee River—the name true to the Cherokee translation, which means "by the river." The lowland stream is broad, shallow,

and pebbly with fine, big trees overhanging its banks. The gravel path curls under the trees, flat for most of the way, although there are some ups and downs. The soft, wide walkway, weaving along the riverbank and then through the woods, is quiet and peaceful, although never far from the main

Mountain Farm Museum at Oconaluftee

highway. All ages walk this pleasant trail, and it is not necessary to have hiking boots or a back pack here.

At about a half mile, the trail passes under the Blue Ridge Parkway and then veers right, away from the stream, to curl into the woods. The trail follows a small creek into a forest of hardwoods and evergreens. It winds appealingly among the trees and soon passes over the creek on a short bridge.

This section of the trail is shady and picturesque. The path rises and falls gently over undulating hills through the woods. You forget you are so near the Newfound Gap Road until you see it to the right of the trail through the trees. At 1.4 miles, the path meets Big Cove Road, which you can cross over the bridge and walk another 0.1 mile further to the trail's end along the river.

To add to your hiking distance, you could walk on down the sidewalk into Cherokee and enjoy puttering in the shops or buying lunch and an ice cream cone before you hike back. The roundtrip hike is only 3 miles long.

Because this is such a short hiking trail, we recommend that you plan to drive over to hike up to Mingo Falls the same day. You will drive across the bridge where Oconaluftee Trail met Big Cove Road and travel 4.5 miles to the Mingo Falls Campground where the falls trail begins.

Lead Cove Trail

Date Hiked: WINTER - March 18th
Mileage: 3.6 miles Roundtrip
Our Rating: Strenuous
Directions: Hwy 321 to Townsend Wye; right on Laurel Creek Road 5.6 miles to parking spaces on right and left of road at trailhead for Lead Cove and other trails in vicinity.
Trail Description:

Lead Cove is a 1.8 miles hike from Laurel Creek Road to the Bote Mountain Trail. The trail gets quite steep on the upper half, and the going will make you "feel" the trail is longer with a rise of 1,200 feet elevation in a short distance. The name of the trail comes from the lead ore once mined from the area to make bullets and ammunition.

The start of Lead Cove Trail begins as a gradual ascent out of Big Spring Cove, a low point along the south side of Laurel Creek Road. The trail soon crosses Sugar Cove Prong, a shallow brook, and then winds uphill along the left of the Prong. Ruins of an old chimney and stone foundation of the Gibson Tipton cabin sit by the trailside at 0.5 mile. There are several scenic spots along this early portion of the trail including picturesque creek scenes, cascades, and little waterfalls bubbling over rocks into pools below. As you hike up Lead Cove, you criss-cross over the stream a time or two as you walk. These are all easy jumps over the rocks as the stream is never broad.
160

The pathway is single-file on Lead Cove, the footing soft and not overly rocky. A wide variety of hardwood and evergreen trees, including chestnut oaks, black cherry, tulip trees and hemlocks shade the way and you will pass thickets of rhododendron, patches of fern, and squawroot. Although March was early for wildflowers, we saw violets and white hepatica on our hike—with the hint of other flowers, like trillium and bloodwort, soon to come.

The trail crosses Laurel Cove Creek further up the way and swings right to follow alongside this creek. Lead Cove Trail begins to climb more steeply now, and soon angles sharply left to

climb away from the creeks and on up the ridge-lines. Thick grapevines twine around some of the trees on the last half mile of the trail. In March, the trees had not fully leafed out, and there were grand views on the latter portion of Lead Cove Trail, looking back eastward toward Rich Mountain and the Chilhowee ranges. The trail ends on a high ridge crest called Sandy Gap where it intersects with the Bote Mountain Trail. At the trail intersection is a nice, flat log for a lunch break—plus more vistas off the Bote Trail over to Defeat Ridge and Thunderhead Mountain.

The return walk back is an easier, downhill hike. For variety, and a longer 7 miles roundtrip hike, you can take a loop-hike return. Hike south 2.5 miles down the Bote Mountain Trail, turn left onto Finley Cane Trail, and hike 2.7 miles back to the parking area where you began.

161

Ramsay Cascades Trail

Date Hiked: SPRING - March 26th
Mileage: 8 miles Roundtrip
Our Rating: Strenuous
Directions: Hwy 441 to Gatlinburg; left on Hwy 321 at Traffic Light #3; right at 6 miles on Greenbrier Road; 3.2 miles to bridge; left at bridge and 1.8 miles to end of road and parking area.
Trail Description:

Although a long, steep, and strenuous hike the beauty of the Ramsay Cascades Trail and the grandeur of the cascades at the trail's end make this trail's popularity in the Smokies understandable. Plan 6 full hours for this hike: approximately 3 hours each for the hike to the falls and return trip and a half hour at the falls for a lunch break and rest. This is no hike for beginners or the health-impaired. The trail rises over 2,220 feet in the four mile trip up to the falls.

The Ramsay Cascades Trail begins at a long bridge over the beautiful cascades of the Middle Prong. The trail next winds its way up a broad, pleasant logging road along the left bank of the Middle Prong for 1.5 miles. Footing is good on this road-bed section and moss-covered logs and beds of dwarf iris lie along the trailside. Manmade benches are frequent, and the uphill ascents are broken by flat landings, an early hallmark of this steep "steps and land-ings" trail.

The Ramsay Cascades Trail follows

Spectacular Ramsay Cascades

through a beautiful forest region for its entire journey, skirting either alongside or near the Middle Prong or Ramsay Prong streams for most of the way. At 1.5 miles, the trail arrives at an open clearing, narrows and turns to follow east beside the Ramsay Prong. Along this trail section, you crisscross the prong and little tributaries several times, twice over long, railed footbridges. You will begin to meet many steep and rocky trail sections at this point where long series of rock stairs test the stamina of your knees and calves. At approximately 2.5 miles, look for "the three sisters"—two especially large virgin tulip poplars with diameters of 5 to 6 feet with the third tulip poplar not far beyond. In this virgin forest area, also watch for other old growth trees, silverbells, giant tulip trees, basswoods, and huge birch trees standing up on tiptoe on their roots. Many of the largest trees in the park grow here.

The last half mile of the Ramsay Trail climbs and curls left up a hillside away from the stream and then winds back to it again. In some seasons wild ramp grow here. The final mile skirting along the Ramsay Prong is an especially arduous climb—up and over rocks, roots, and steps, and in and out of narrow passages between large rock boulders—before arriving, at last, to the base of the falls. Ramsay Cascades, one of the highest falls in the park, is a spectacular broad 100 foot waterfall display, tumbling over and down a high rock ledge. Many smooth, giant boulders sprawl around the base of the falls to spread a picnic on. The roaring cascades and pools are very beautiful, and you will want to linger before starting the long hike back.

Maddron Bald/Albright Grove

Date Hiked: SPRING - April 10th
Mileage: 7.6 miles Roundtrip
Our Rating: Moderate - Strenuous
Directions: Hwy 441 to Gatlinburg; left on Hwy 321 N at Traffic Light #3; 16 miles to first right past Yogi Bear Campground to quick right on Laurel Springs to roadside parking at trailhead.
Trail Description:

This is a difficult trailhead to find if you are unfamiliar with the Smoky Mountain area. However, the walk up Maddron Bald to Albright Grove Nature

Trail is worth the hunt for the side roads that lead to the trailhead. Albright Grove, named after early park director Horace Albright, is a picture-book piece of virgin forest, thought to hold some of the southeast's oldest trees.

You will find parking on the roadsides at the start of the Maddron Bald Trail. The trail begins just behind a park gate and starts an uphill march on a broad graveled roadbed. It's a steep climb here, rising up the back ridges of Maddron Bald between Snag Mountain and Buckeye Lead. Old settlements once lay alongside this road, and at 1.5 miles on the right of the trail is the one-room Baxter Cabin built in the late 1800s that you can explore. Soon after, the road crosses Cole Creek and follows beside it almost a mile to a wide intersection at approximately 1.2 miles from the start of the trail.

This is a fine spot to rest. Gabes Mountain Trail goes west, Old Settlers Trail swings east, and Maddron Bald proceeds straight ahead between two rock boulders. The graveled road trail now narrows to a more rustic, soft-footed wagon road. This part of the trail is more pleasant than the earlier trail section— a nice, moderate walk through open woods with many tall, straight tulip poplars down the hillsides. At 2.3 miles the trail comes to a fork. Take the right path here. The trail now starts a delightful deep woods walk into old virgin forest. In April, wildflowers were scattered under the trees and among the ferns along the

way—trillium, yellow trout lily, Fraser's sedge, spring beauty, violets, bluets, chickweed, and hepatica. As you begin to see huge hemlocks, maples, and beech trees, you will hear Indian Creek down on the right below you. Soon the trail crosses this creek on a long foot bridge at 2.7 miles. This is a beautiful spot for a picnic or rest on big boulders beside the cascades and pools in the stream.

At 2.9 miles, the Albright Grove Loop Trail turns right. The loop trail adds 0.7 mile to your overall hike but shouldn't be missed. The loop is a special walk though massive trees and a wonderland forest. Here, some of the ancient trees—poplars and hemlocks—have diameters up to 25 feet in circumference. The deep, shady woods is alive with flowers, birdsong, fern, red squirrels, and mosses. The loop curls around and back to the Maddron Bald Trail. To return at this point provides a 6.8 miles roundtrip hike. We enjoyed hiking another 0.4 mile up Maddron Bald Trail to a second crossing of Indian Creek before turning back to start the downhill return to our car for a 7.6 miles roundtrip journey.

Lakeshore/Fontana Trail

Date Hiked: SPRING - April 16th
Mileage: 8 miles Roundtrip
Our Rating: Moderate
Directions: Hwy 321 from Maryville to right on Foothills Parkway; left on Hwy 129 over mountain to Deals Gap; then left on Hwy 28 and on to left turn up road to Fontana Dam parking area.
Trail Description:

The Lakeshore Trail is a 16.6 miles maze of interconnected trails and old roads curling along between the southern foothills of the Smokies and Fontana Lake. Before Fontana Dam and the lake were created, the backhills of the Smokies and the Lakeshore region were well-populated and widely enjoyed for

recreation by locals and travelers. Now, there is only walking access to these beautiful regions from the Fontana and Bryson City ends of the area.

We had planned a more lengthy hiking exploration of the Lakeshore Trail at Fontana, but the road that goes over the dam was closed for construction. So we added approximately a mile to our hike walking from the parking lot over the dam to get to the trailhead. After crossing the dam, the pathway forks right to travel 0.6 mile to an intersection of Shuckstack Trail on the left—a steep and arduous 3.5 miles climb leading up to the Shuckstack Lookout Tower. A short distance beyond the trail split Lakeshore Trail begins at a clear park sign.

The Lakeshore Trail starts as a broad trail, but later narrows to a single-file path that curls in and out along the ridgelines on the back flank of Shuckstack Mountain. The west end of the Lakeshore Trail coils up behind a finger of Fontana Lake, but there are only a few points where you can see the water down through the woods. One of these is at 0.5 mile at an abrupt left turning in the trail.

There are often artifacts and evidence along the Lakeshore Trail of the settlements that once lay scattered through this area. Rock formations also remind you that copper, silver, and other ores were once mined from the region. The Lakeshore Trail is an undulating walk, never rising up into the mountains behind it. The path often is very narrow, hugging the sides of the slopes and then curling back into the woods to cross little rills or streams. At about 1 mile is an especially picturesque crossing of Payne Branch. Then, the trail coils in and out again as it rises up the ridgelines to an open gap on Shuckstack Ridge. After climbing down the ridge, the trail angles sharply left again, giving occasional peeks down to Eagle Creek inlet along the way. At 2.5 miles is a creek crossing and just past the 3 miles point is a broader stream crossing, at Birchfield Branch, where we turned around to start our return. For a longer hike, walk a mile further to the intersection of Twentymile Trail and rocky Campsite #90 on the banks of Eagle Creek. When the dam road is open, this makes a fine 8 miles roundtrip hike.

Rough Fork Trail

Date Hiked: SPRING - April 23rd
Mileage: 6 miles Roundtrip
Our Rating: Moderate - Strenuous
Directions: I-40 to NC Exit 20; 0.2 mile to right on Cove Creek Road; follow this gravel road to intersection with paved road; then left approximately 4-5 miles to end of road and trailhead.
Trail Description:

Rough Fork Trail starts at the end of the scenic Cataloochee Valley. This green valley, tucked between the surrounding mountain ranges is very similar to Cades Cove but smaller and less known. You will pass restored cabins, a church, and a schoolhouse on your route back to the trailhead. All these buildings are on the National Register of Historic Places.

There is a nice level parking area where the trail begins. Rough Fork starts behind a gate and follows along Rough Fork Creek. The trail in the early section is broad, the way flat, and this part of the trail is easy enough for all the family to

hike. The woods are open and quiet along the way with scatterings of wildflowers and many butterflies in spring. The hiking trail crisscrosses Rough Fork Creek over four footbridges along the first one and a half mile section of the way, each a scenic spot to stop and enjoy.

At about 1 mile, after crossing the third footbridge, you will see the historic S. L. Woody house set in a pretty clearing to the left of the trail. The house, built in the 1800s, is well maintained and also has a remaining springhouse. Stop to take a look around before walking on. You can go inside the house, and if you like, picnic on the grounds. Beyond the Woody house, and shortly after the fourth creek crossing of Hurricane Creek at 1.5 miles, the trail splits in a small intersection. Angling to the right is a short trail leading 1.5 miles over to Campsite #40, a pleasant side hike. To continue on the Rough Fork Trail, stay to the left after you cross the bridge.

Where the first 1.5 miles of Rough Fork was an easy to moderate walk, the next 1.5 miles is a steep, hard climb and a more strenuous hike. This second section of the trail is narrow, often hugging the ridgelines with steep drop-offs on the left of the trail. The hardwoods are pretty on this upper section of the trail—with maples, beech, oaks, and yellow birch shading the way. In April when we hiked, there were many wildflowers along the trail. We saw yellow and white trillium, brook lettuce, sedge and wood betony, and yellow buttercups. We even spotted a jack-in-the pulpit on the day we hiked. At 2.7 miles the trail reaches a gap at the top of Big Fork Ridge. The trail then ascends slightly through a rhododendron thicket until it reaches the intersection of Caldwell Fork Trail at 3 miles. This is a good place to turn around and start back.

Historic S.L. Woody House

Huskey Gap Trail

Date Hiked: SPRING - May 7th
Mileage: 6 miles Roundtrip
Our Rating: Strenuous
Directions: Hwy 441 through Gatlinburg and continue approximately 1.7 miles past Sugarlands Visitor Center; trailhead is on right but park on left near path marked "2nd Quiet Walkway."
Trail Description:

The start of the Huskey Gap Trail is just over a mile and a half from the

Visitor's Center. Parking for the hike is on the left across the street from the trailhead at the 2nd Quiet Walkway. The Sugarlands Valley Nature Trail and another Quiet Walkway are also on the left before the Huskey Gap Trail, so watch carefully-not to miss the park area and start of the

trail. You may also want to explore the three short nature walks while in the area, as each are scenic and less than a mile roundtrip in length.

After parking at the nature trail, walk directly across Newfound Gap Road to the start of Huskey Gap Trail. There is a rustic trail sign at the start of the hike. Huskey Gap climbs 2 miles up to the top of Sugarland Mountain and then 2 miles down the other side to meet the Little River Trail coming out of Elkmont. The first 2 miles is a strenuous uphill trudge, gaining over 1,000 feet of elevation, but it passes through a pleasant, shady hardwood forest. Along the climb up, you hop across shallow Flint Rock Branch, walk by interesting boulder fields, and see grapevines hanging from the trees. Some of the tulip poplars along the trail have vast diameters you cannot even wrap your arms around. In the springtime, this section of the Huskey Gap Trail is also alive with wildflowers. April to early May is the peak time, usually, for trillium in the Smokies, and if you can hike Huskey Gap then you will see nearly every trillium variety in rich abundance along this one hike. Along the trailside and hillsides in early May we also saw purple wild geranium and phacelia, riots of white Canadian violets, rue-anemone, delicate bishops cap, thick patches of wild dwarf iris, purple phlox, white bloodroot, chickweed, and Solomon's seal.

Wild yellow stonecrop was in bloom in crevices in the rocks and white may-apples were in flower under broad umbrella leaves.

After rising 2 miles up the slopes of Sugarland Mountain, the Huskey Gap Trail meets the Sugarland Mountain Trail at an open, mountaintop clearing called the Huskey Gap. At this intersection, you can turn around and return for a 4 miles roundtrip hike or extend your walk by hiking further along Huskey Gap as it starts down the mountain on the other side. We recommend hiking another mile to the stream crossing at Phoebe Branch, where you will find rushing cascades, enormous rock boulders, and a nice rest bench to have your lunch on before turning back.

Cosby Creek Trail

Date Hiked: SPRING - May 14th
Mileage: 4 miles Roundtrip
Our Rating: Easy
Directions: I-40 to Exit 443 at Foothills Parkway; follow Parkway into Hwy 321/32; stay on Hwy 32 to road to Cosby Campground; follow road 3 miles to end and hiker parking.
Trail Description:

The Cosby Creek Trail is marked only by a sign reading "Horse Trail," but many hikers and walkers enjoy this easy, pleasant woods trail winding along the Cosby Creek. It is unlikely that you will find this nice trail written up in any other hiking book accounts. However, the trail is not difficult to find.

After parking at the Cosby Campground Hiker Parking area, walk up the Campground Road to the head of Lower Mt Cammerer Trail to the left. The entrance to this trail is well-marked. Follow this wide roadbed trail for approximately 0.2 mile to a footlog crossing of Cosby Creek. After the creek crossing you will come to an open intersection of several trails. A trail sign for Low Gap Trail is on the right of the intersection, and a smaller sign simply marked Horse Trail is on the left. This is the beginning of the Cosby Creek Trail. Turn left and start your hike here.

Cosby Creek is an undulating woods trail with soft rises and falls that any novice hiker can enjoy. The trail runs for 2 miles northeast through the woods below Sutton Ridge and Wildcat Knob, frequently skirting alongside the east bank of the tumbling Cosby Creek. The trail follows a path nearly parallel to the paved road, and occasionally bits of the Cosby picnic area and roadway are visible through the trees on your hike. The early part of the trail leads back into a shady forest of hardwoods and evergreens with fern, flowers, and mushrooms scattered along the way. In season, there are wildflowers and flowering dogwoods here, too. Shortly, the trail weaves in toward the Cosby Creek and crosses it. It is easy to cross the creek on well-placed boulders in the stream, and the water around the rocks is not very deep.

Over the next mile and a half of the Cosby Trail, the trail will wander in from the woods to cross Cosby Creek, and then Toms Creek, about five more times. In most spots the streams are very shallow, needing only a few rock-hops to get across. In two places, the crossings are a little broader. However, much of the charm of this trail is in its pattern of meandering in and out from the woods to the creeks. Each crossing is a new, small adventure. We saw many family groups on this trail, particularly in the early part of the trail nearer the campground area. The hike ends at a scenic creek-side spot with cascades very near the road. We looked for a possible continuation of the trail on the other side of the creek, but couldn't find one, so we turned around at this point to return.

Crib Gap Trail

Date Hiked: SPRING - May 21st
Mileage: 4 miles Roundtrip
Our Rating: Easy/Moderate
Directions: Hwy 321 to Townsend Wye; right on Laurel Creek Road; continue on 5.8 miles to trailhead and parking on the right.

Trail Description:

To get to the beginning of Crib Gap Trail, you start by hiking 0.2 mile down the Turkeypen Ridge Trail. Turkeypen starts out of an area called Big Spring Cove and curls back into the woods towards Turkeypen Ridge and Scott Mountain. There is a clear trail marker on the right side of the Laurel Creek Road. Crib Gap Trail veers left off Turkeypen Ridge at a small clearing shortly up the path. Crib Gap was once one of the many settlers' roads connecting farms in this area over to those closer to Cades Cove.

The early part of Crib Gap Trail is a short, but enjoyable, walk through a pleasant woods. It is easy to imagine the cabins and farms that used to exist in the open areas along this trail. Often, you can see remains of side roads that once led to home sites or barns on the early section of this trail. The hike is mostly soft under foot and flat, with easy walking, with only a few rocky sections to navigate. At several points along the trail trickley rills, or small streamlets, run across the pathway. If it has been raining heavily in the Smokies, these patches can be muddy and slick.

Toward the end of the first mile, Crib Gap begins to curl left and climb a more wooded hillside. The forest is thicker here, with maples and other hardwoods, flowering dogwoods, and hemlock. This is also a good place to see deer, squirrels, and chipmunks. Soon, the trail comes to Laurel Creek Road and crosses it to pick up the trail on the other side.

On this second stretch of Crib Gap Trail, the hike changes flavor and character. It climbs into a forested hillside, becoming a more narrow, rutted, and rocky walk. The trail winds its way upward and around the ridge to come to an open clearing and high point. Here you can look down on the road and the Crib Gap area below. The trail then turns and begins a gradual descent toward the Anthony Creek Trail. This is a pretty section of the hike. In May, look for flowering mountain shrubs like laurel and rhododendron, and spring wildflowers. We saw bright, red fire pinks, purple phacelia, yellow trillium, and even a clump of showy orchis by an old log. You may see several varieties of mushrooms and butterflies also.

The trail ends into Anthony Creek Trail. The Cades Cove picnic area is less than a half-mile to the right down Anthony Creek. The picnic area has nice tables, restrooms, and water fountains. Turn right to get to the picnic area and have your lunch by the stream before starting the hike back over Crib Gap Trail and Turkeypen to return to your car.

We came upon two deer feeding in this clearing.

175

Flat Creek Trail

Date Hiked: SPRING - June 11th

Mileage: 6.6 miles Roundtrip

Our Rating: Moderate

Directions: Hwy 441 over Newfound Gap and down the mountain; left onto Blue Ridge Parkway approximately 0.5 mile past Oconaluftee Visitor Center; after 8 miles turn left on Hientooga Road; follow approximately 4 miles to pullover on left at trailhead.

Trail Description:

Allow extra travel time to drive over the mountains and up the Blue Ridge Parkway to get to the Balsam Mountain area of the Smokies. The turn sign off the Blue Ridge Parkway says "Balsam Mountain and Black Camp Gap" rather than Heintooga Road. The south end of the Flat Creek Trail is on the left side of the road after several miles. Although most hiking books write up the trail starting from the north end, we recommend starting at the south end so that most of the uphill climb of the hike is on the walk in and not back out.

For beauty and an idyllic hike, Flat Creek can hardly be surpassed. The trail is a narrow, winding one with moderate ups and downs between long flat stretches of woodland. The beginning of the trail drops down first to cross Flat Creek at 0.5 mile on a log bridge, and then rolls up and down the ridgelines, crossing Bunches Creek on a second bridge at approximately 0.7 mile. The trail then moves through a forest of maple, birch, and rhododendron with occasional views to the south toward Soco Bald and Barnett Knob.

At one mile up the trail is a marked spur trail for Flat Creek Falls leading off to the left. This side trail weaves about 0.5 mile down to the falls, which is

really a layered grouping of rolling cascades spilling downhill in the stream. When the spur trail splits, take the right fork over to the upper cascades. The left trail fork leads downstream below the cascades and the footing on this path is treacherous. A better way to get to the lower falls is to rock-hop or wade over the stream above the upper falls to the trail leading down the other side. The lower cascade section has a chute rock falls in it.

After returning to the main path, Flat Creek Trail continues north to culminate at the Balsam Mountain Campground. The trail then rises uphill through the woods and between lush sections of trailside grasses. It crosses Flat Creek on log bridges three times in the next half-mile or so, often passing through old growth forest and rhododendron thickets. This is a very scenic section of the trail. At 2 miles Flat Creek Trail arrives at a rough trail junction. An old trail used to lead from this point back to Bunches Creek Road in the Indian Reservation, but it is no longer maintained. Continue your hike north to arrive at the back end of the Campground. There are picnic tables, water fountains, and a restroom here for a break before you start back. You may want to take the short trail out of the north end of the parking lot to Heintooga Mile High Overlook from which you can see spectacular views of the Smokies ranges at 5,250 feet.

Noland Creek Trail

Date Hiked: SUMMER - August 6th
Mileage: 8 miles Roundtrip
Our Rating: Moderate
Directions: Hwy 441 over Newfound Gap to Cherokee; right on Hwy 19; right on Everett to cross the river into Bryson City; stay left onto Lakeview Drive to parking at bridge over Noland Creek.
Trail Description:

Noland Creek is one of several trails branching off near the end of the old Lakeview Drive which is called "The Road to Nowhere." The road was begun by the park service in the 1940s to travel behind Fontana Lake from Bryson City to Fontana Dam. The new road was intended to reopen access to the back of the Smokies which the dam and new lake had made inaccessible. However, funding ran short, controversy developed, and the project was abandoned, leaving only a section of the promised highway behind. You will see some bitter signs still standing along the roadside.

Noland Creek Trail begins just before the bridge crossing of Noland Creek about 1 mile before the end of "The Road to Nowhere." You will see a parking area to the left side of the road just before the bridge. Park here and follow the pathway downhill to an intersection. Turn right to start your hike. The left trail only travels down a short mile to a campsite area.

All of the first 5 miles of Noland Creek Trail follow along a broad, soft-footed wagon road on which two hikers can easily walk side by side. At 0.5 mile the trail goes under the Highway and then crosses Noland Creek on a wide, wooden bridge. This is one of several creek crossings along the trail. The roadbed

then winds gradually uphill through a primarily hardwood forest, with the Noland Creek never far from the trailside. Watch for a boulder field and a spring alongside the path in the first mile up the trail. At approximately 1.5 miles, a side trail leads left to wander up Bearpen Branch for less than a quarter mile to reach Campsite #65. This is a nice spot for a rest or lunch at the picnic tables here.

Back on the main path, Noland Creek Trail continues to climb gently up the south side of the Smokies through a valley between Forney Ridge and Noland Divide. Between 2 to 2.5 miles the trail comes to another creek crossing and a clearing, a picturesque spot where Noland Creek rushes in foamy cascades over a series of rocks. Past this point, the trail enters a forested area of white pines. Along this trail section, you will see settlement relics and evidence of sites where mountain homes once stood. Look for rock steps and boxwoods settlers once planted along front walkways leading to their cabins. Where Horse Cove Creek meets the Noland Creek you will even see ornamental yucca plants.

At 3.1 miles, another wood bridge crosses the Noland Creek. In the next half mile are some nice mountain views out over the creek. At the 4 miles point, you will arrive at a creek crossing of Mill Creek over a large bridge and then at Campsite #64, where we rested before turning around to hike back. There are picnic tables at this nice campsite by the stream and Springhouse Branch Trail comes in from the left.

The Jumpoff

Date Hiked: SUMMER - August 31st
Mileage: 6.8 miles Roundtrip
Our Rating: Strenuous
Directions: Hwy 441 to Newfound Gap Road to the parking lot at Newfound Gap at the top of the mountain; the trail starts to the far left of the parking lot.

Trail Description:

    The hike to the Jumpoff follows a popular, heavily used piece of the Appalachian Trail. With this in mind, try to plan your hike on a weekday or off season to avoid the crowds or in mild weather when there have been no recent snows or

rains. This is a very narrow, rutted out trail with exposed roots and many rocks to climb over and around. The trail ices in winter and gets nasty and muddy after heavy rains, becoming dangerous due to the steep drop-offs on either side of the trail. At any season, this trail is strenuous and taxing—and not a good choice for a novice hiker or anyone with knee or foot problems.

    After a short, steady walk to begin this trail, the path quickly becomes narrow and steep and begins to climb. On the high ridges here are spruce, fir, beech and other hardy, high altitude trees. The trail climbs 300 feet in the first half mile and 200 more in the second. Wonderful views begin to open up on the right side

of the trail right away, and later on the left. Care needs to be taken with your footing at all times, since the trail works around exposed rocks, sharp narrow curves, and exposed tree roots. There are many places where you have to climb and clamber over boulders in the path. At a mile up the trail, watch for blackberry bushes, and at about 1.5

miles look for a pleasant open stretch with a side trail leading left to a great view of Mount Le Conte and Peregrine Peak. At 1.7 miles you arrive at the intersection where Sweat Heifer Trail angles in from the right, having curled and climbed up the back of the mountain from Kephart Prong below. There is a marvelous old, knarled tree here at the Sweat Heifer intersection, and it is advisable to take a rest at this point before heading on up the trail again. Before leaving the intersection, walk 0.2 mile down Sweat Heifer to see a spectacular view of the mountains.

The next section is the steepest of the hike but opens to several more majestic views off the crest of the mountain. At about 2.5 miles the trail finally moves into a wooded, undulating, and easier walking section before intersecting with the Boulevard Trail on the left at 2.7 miles. Turn left on the Boulevard Trail for approximately 0.5 mile and then right at the trail sign to the Jumpoff. Then get ready to climb and scramble up a stony, ravined path. The rough pathway twines up and over the ridge and down a steep, rock-strewn trail before coming to a bald, or open field, atop Mount Kephart at 3.2 miles. This is a nice place to spread a lunch and rest. The Jumpoff is the name for the cliffs here on the side of Mount Kephart, which drop off in a rocky, 1,000-foot precipice down the side of the mountain. Despite the name, don't Jump Off!!! And don't get too close to the edge of the cliffs as the rocks are loose and shaley, the soil eroding. On a clear day the gorgeous views off the Jumpoff toward Charlies Bunion, Horseshoe Mountain, and down the valley below make this taxing hike truly worthwhile.

Scenic mountain views along the Appalachian Trail

181

Big Fork Ridge Trail

Date Hiked: SUMMER - September 3rd
Mileage: 6.2 miles Roundtrip
Our Rating: Moderate
Directions: I-40 to NC Exit 20; 0.2 mile to right on Cove Creek Road; follow this gravel road to intersection with paved road; left and approximately 4-5 miles to end of road and trailhead.
Trail Description:

Big Fork Ridge Trail climbs up from the Cataloochee Valley across Big Fork Ridge and then down the other side to Caldwell Fork Creek. The trail begins at the back end of the Cataloochee Valley.

The hike starts to the left of the parking area by crossing Rough Fork Creek on a long foot-bridge. It then begins a gradual, steady ascent up Big Fork Ridge through a deep, shaded forest

filled with red maple trees—glorious in the fall. Shortly after the bridge crossing, look for a wide, open field, which was once the site of the Caldwell homestead. This family once owned over 150 acres in the valley and a stream, ridge, and trail are named

182

after them. You will also see a wooden enclosure in this area used by the park to keep elk secure before their release.

As you hike the first mile of Big Fork Ridge, watch for some vast hemlock trees in this old growth forest. In the spring, wildflowers and dogwoods bloom in profusion on the early trail and mountain laurel and rhododendron flower in dense thickets on the upper trail. Toward the end of the first mile, you will cross several stream rivulets running across the trail. In rainy weather, these and the horse traffic in the area make this trail muddy, rutted, and less comfortable to hike.

At one mile the trail angles sharply to the right. The ongoing path rolls up and down around the ridgeline for about a half mile before it reaches the high point of the trail on Big Fork Ridge at 1.8 miles. Two old horse hitches sit beside the trail at the gap. You have climbed about 600 feet up from the valley now and you may hear the Rough Fork Creek far below you on this stretch of your hike. The trail flattens out for about a half mile on the top of the ridge before starting downhill at 2 miles. The woods continue to be lush and green here, with large Fraser magnolia and another stream rivulet to cross. Watch for an open area in the trees on the left where you can catch a nice view down into the valley below.

At 2.5 miles, the trail switches back to the right toward Rabbit Ridge and comes to a clearing. The old Caldwell Fork Schoolhouse used to be on this site, as there were once enough settlers in Cataloochee to support several schools. Continuing down the ridge, you will begin to hear the Caldwell Fork stream below and come to a foot-bridge crossing of this tumbling stream at 2.7 miles. The path only climbs up from the creek another 100 yards or so further before it ends into the Caldwell Fork Trail. This scenic crossing at the stream is a nice place to stop for a rest and a lunch before starting the return hike up and over the ridge once more to return to your car.

Road Prong Trail

Date Hiked: SUMMER - September 10th
Mileage: 4.8 miles Roundtrip
Our Rating: Strenuous
Directions: Hwy 441 thru Gatlinburg up Newfound Gap Road; turn right on Clingmans Dome Road and drive approximately 1 mile to Indian Gap parking area on right.
Trail Description:

The Road Prong Trail starts out of Indian Gap and follows what was once a part of the Indians' and settlers' main wagon route over the Smoky Mountains. The narrow forest trail drops 2.4 miles steeply downhill, twisting in and out of the streambeds, to intersect the Chimney Tops Trail far below.

From the parking area off the Clingmans Dome Road, walk north through a grassy field to the trailhead sign to begin your hike. The trail quickly crosses the Appalachian Trail and then begins its descent on a rocky, steep pathway. The trail often seems to be picking its way through a rough, washed out streambed. Road Prong is not a good hike for beginners, but the forest it weaves through is beautiful, with tall majestic hemlocks, Christmas fir trees, green ferns, and lush mosses.

At approximately 0.5 mile down the trail, you can hear the early head-waters of the Road Prong off to the left. The stream will broaden and strengthen as it spills down the mountain. At approximately 1 mile, you rock-hop the Road Prong for the first time before swinging right to hike past a clogged, pool area in the creek. Then, you skinny down a steep bank to cross the Prong again, before angling left to twine up and down the creek bank to yet another crossing. At this

point, the trail begins to literally follow in and out of the streambed through a deep valley for the next half mile. It's a somewhat treacherous stretch where you need to jump from rock to rock or simply walk in the stream. Finally, at approximately 1.5 miles, the trail climbs away from the creek briefly before returning to it again near "Talking Falls." You can scramble down to the base of the falls with effort.

The next crossing of the Road Prong is at Standing Rock Ford. Look for the actual Standing Rock formation that the ford is named after before crossing the stream. It is a big, pointed rock to the right of the trail. The stream has gained size and strength now, tumbling in cascades through a deep gorge below the trail. As you walk on, watch for another waterfall, called "Trickling Falls," far below on the right.

The last section of the hiking trail continues in a steep, harsh, and rocky descent. Try to imagine a pioneer wagon getting down this trail as you work your way over its rock ledges, washed out ruts, and exposed tree roots. In the last half mile, the Road Prong Trail moves into a relatively flat section called Indian Grave Flats, before descending again to the end of the trail at an open trail intersection called Beech Flats. The return hike is an all-uphill climb and even more strenuous than the hike down. You can shorten the overall hike by hiking 1.8 miles out to a 2nd car at the Chimneys parking lot.

Mt. Collins Trail

Date Hiked: SUMMER - September 17th
Mileage: 6.5 miles Roundtrip
Our Rating: Strenuous
Directions: Hwy 441 through Gatlinburg up to Newfound Gap; turn right on Clingmans Dome Road and drive approximately 1 mile to Indian Gap parking area on right.
Trail Description:

This trail is another accessible piece of the Applachian Trail, which crosses the top ranges of the Smoky Mountains. Many of the Appalachian Trail sections have their own local trail names, like this one. The Mt. Collins Trail climbs 3.5 miles up the Appalachian Trail, from Indian Gap at 5,250 feet to Mt. Collins at 6,188 feet, gaining 938 feet in its southwest journey. The trail is a somewhat rocky and steep trail but a very unique and memorable one.

The trailhead begins to the left of the parking area at Indian Gap and winds sharply upward for over a mile with only occasional relief. There are many log steps built into this section of the trail by the park service, as well as natural stone and rock steps. You hike a little, climb some steps, hike a little more, and climb some more steps throughout the first mile, giving the legs and knees a good workout. As you climb, you will catch vistas to the right out over the mountain ranges of Sugarland Mountain.

At approximately 1 mile, the trail begins to descend and then rises again to enter a spruce/fir forest. The trail is narrow and enchanting here—like a Christmas tree forest all around. The smell of the evergreens is fresh and pun-

gent, and the thick multitude of Christmas trees of all sizes and shapes is unexpectedly delightful. The pathway levels off for a space in this section, a nice relief in your forest walk, and crosses a little trickley rill on a log bridge. After the bridge, at approximately 2.5 miles up the trail, watch for a trailside bench on the left, a nice rest spot and picnic site.

At 2.7 miles, the trail hits a junction with Fork Ridge Trail, which leads left back to Clingmans Dome Road. A little further up the trail at 3 miles Sugarland Mountain Trail intersects on the right. Look for a huge quartz rock near the intersection that is big enough to sit on. You can take a side trip, if desired, down the Sugarland Mountain Trail to the Mt. Collins shelter. Hike approximately 0.5 mile down Sugarland, and take the side trail for about 50 yards to the 12-bunk shelter.

From the Sugarland Trail intersection, at Fighting Gap, it is only about a half mile further uphill to reach the high point of Mt. Collins. The last half-mile is a sharp climb, with more log steps, that winds up through a scenic forest. A level section marks the high point on the trail, and there are nice views to the north out across the mountain ranges here. The return hike back to your car is a more comfortable, downhill walk.

Russell Field Trail

Date Hiked: FALL - September 24th
Mileage: 9.2 miles Roundtrip
Our Rating: Moderate/Strenuous
Directions: Hwy 321 to Townsend Wye; right on Laurel Creek Road to left at Cades Cove picnic area; park at back of picnic area at trailhead.
Trail Description:

    The hike up to Russell Field Trail begins at the back end of the Cades Cove Picnic area and climbs to the well-known Russell Field bald. On busy weekends, parking here is a challenge. The first 1.6 miles of the hike follows

the Anthony Creek Trail, a scenic, woods trail wandering up the streamside and over several bridges before reaching a trail junction where Russell Field turns right. You will find some large rest rocks in this wide intersection under tall tulip trees—a nice spot for a break.

    As soon as you begin your hike up the Russell Field Trail, you can see and hear the Left Prong stream below on your right. The pathway climbs steadily upward for 3.5 miles, gaining 2,000 feet in elevation, before meeting the Appalachian Trail. The hike is steep, from beginning to end, with no flat sections of trail for relief, so you might need to stop occasionally to rest as you climb.

    The first quarter mile of the trail angles sharply uphill alongside the Left Prong. The path is soft under foot as it moves beneath the trees, and the stream is never far away. Early on the trail are several shallow creek crossings and many views down on the Prong to beautiful pools and cascades. Watch for a tumbling waterfall with a deep pool as you move up the trail—and in late June and early July glorious rhododendron.

After a quarter-mile, the trail moves into a deep, idyllic virgin forest missed by the loggers. Lush ferns grow thick along the trailsides and large moss-covered rocks decorate the pathway, making this forest area very magical and "elfin." At 0.75 mile, Campsite #10 sits on the right in

a clearing with hewn campsite logs you can rest on. After the campsite, the trail continues its ascent up Leadbetter Ridge along the stream, passing a rock ledge on the left covered in moss and flowers and several pretty cascades and pools on the right. At approximately 2 miles the trail reaches the crest of Leadbetter Ridge to travel less steeply across the ridge top for about a half mile before starting a final 0.5 mile to the hike's destination.

At 3 miles you finally arrive at the edge of Russell Field, one of the high open crests in the Smokies. The views are spectacular off the ridge top and this is a perfect spot for lunch before your return. In early summer,

pink and white mountain laurel bloom in profusion on the bald making the long climb worthwhile. Another half mile takes you across the bald to the trail's end at the Appalachian Trail.

Deep Creek Trail

Date Hiked: FALL - October 28th

Mileage: 6 miles Roundtrip

Our Rating: Moderate

Directions: Hwy 441 over the mountain to Cherokee, NC; turn right on Hwy 19 to Ela; right on Galbraith Creek Road to trailhead at back of Deep Creek Campground.

Trail Description:

Deep Creek Trail begins at a clearly marked trail sign at the back of the Deep Creek Campground on the North Carolina side of the Smokies. Allow extra planning time for the trip over the mountain to the start of this hike—ap-

proximately two hours from the Knoxville or Maryville areas and an hour and 15 minutes from Gatlinburg—but don't let the travel time deter you from driving over to this delightful trail and area in the Great Smoky Mountains.

The hiking trail begins on the left of Deep Creek stream and follows along beside the stream for as many miles as you care to walk. The first two miles of the trail follow a broad, soft-footed roadbed. The ascent is mostly gradual, the path flat and level, and you can walk two-by-two and stretch out your legs for a good-paced walk. Children and the elderly enjoy the early section of this trail. In the first half mile, you will pass Tom Branch Falls on the right of the trail. The falls is easy to spot, since there is a rest bench beside the path at its site. The narrow waterfall cascades picturesquely for 80 feet down a rocky wall on the opposite side of the stream. Beyond the Tom Branch Falls, the trail continues winding up the open settler's road through a fine hardwood forest, coming to an intersection with Indian Creek Trail at 0.7 mile.

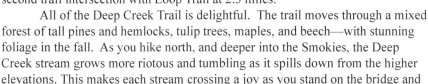

Past the junction Deep Creek Trail continues to meander in an undulating pattern up and down along the creek side. The trail crosses Deep Creek several times on well-constructed wood bridges as it gradually ascends up the south side of the mountain. There will be four bridge crossings before Deep Creek meets the second trail intersection with Loop Trail at 2.3 miles.

All of the Deep Creek Trail is delightful. The trail moves through a mixed forest of tall pines and hemlocks, tulip trees, maples, and beech—with stunning foliage in the fall. As you hike north, and deeper into the Smokies, the Deep Creek stream grows more riotous and tumbling as it spills down from the higher elevations. This makes each stream crossing a joy as you stand on the bridge and

look down on the cascades and pools below. In warm weather, you can climb down beside the bridges to wade in the cold mountain water, rock-hop on the giant boulders in the stream, and maybe spot a trout.

There will be three more bridge crossings after the Loop Trail intersection. Beyond this point at 2.3 miles, the trail begins to narrow, winding up and over a steep ridge before dropping down to arrive at Campsite #60 beside the creek at 3 miles. There is another footbridge here and a long,

flat camping area along the creek. This is a wonderful place to picnic and explore before turning around to return.

Indian Grave Gap Trail

Date Hiked: FALL - October 30th

Mileage: 7.2 miles Roundtrip

Our Rating: Strenuous

Directions: Hwy 321 to Townsend Wye; right on Laurel Creek Road into Cades Cove to right up one-way Rich Mountain Road approximately 1.3 miles to trailhead and parking on right.

Trail Description:

The trailhead for Indian Grave Gap Trail is on the right side of primitive, one-way Rich Mountain Road out of Cades Cove. Follow Cades Cove Road to Rich Mountain Road across from the old Missionary Baptist Church. Drive up the narrow road approximately 2 miles to a pull-over parking area by the trailhead. After your hike, drive over the mountain and down the other side into Tuckaleechee Cove in Townsend.

The Indian Grave Gap Trail begins behind a gate and first winds up an old settlers' roadbed above Tater Ridge. Fall is a gorgeous time to do this hike. The pathway is soft under foot and strewn with fall leaves you can kick through, like a kid, as you walk. The fall foliage in the hardwood forest is breathtaking, with many lovely vistas down through the hills and valleys of the cove and more to distant mountain ranges as you climb. In summer, wildflowers grow along the trailside.

The first section of the trail is a steep climb of 1.1 miles to Indian Grave Gap and the intersection with the Rich Mountain Loop Trail on the right.

This is the sharpest grade on your hike. Shortly after the gap watch for a nice panorama into the cove on your right as the trail winds along Double Mountain below the Rich Mountain ridges above. The next 0.8 mile is more rolling with some relief in its ascent, as the pathway travels up to the Rich Mountain Trail intersection.

At 1.9 miles, the trail broadens into this wide, open junction with Rich Mountain Trail, swinging in from the left. There are more views at this junction of the cove, plus several logs to stop and rest on before hiking on. The trail has gained over 1,000 feet of elevation since its beginning now, and will add over 2,600 feet more before rising to 3,686 feet at Cerulean Knob, the high point of the hike.

  The last section of the trail, from the Rich Mountain intersection to the end of the hike at Scott Mountain Trail, is a more moderate journey. You are walking across the ridgelines of Rich Mountain and Scott Mountain in this 1.7 miles section of the trail. At approximately 0.5 mile past the intersection watch on the left for the side path leading up to Cerulean Knob and the remains of the old Rich Mountain fire tower. Take the short path uphill to the former tower site. Once stupendous views could be seen from this high point, but now the trees have grown to obstruct them. After returning to the main trail, the ongoing path is an easy pleasant walk with many views out over the cove and valley. At the trail's end into Scott Mountain Trail, it is 3.6 miles back to your car, a 7.2 miles roundtrip hike.

Wolf Ridge Trail

Date Hiked: FALL - November 12th
Mileage: 5 miles Roundtrip
Our Rating: Moderate/Strenuous
Directions: Hwy 321 from Maryville to right on Foothills Parkway to end of Parkway: left on Hwy 129 to Deals Gap onto Hwy 28; turn left at Twentymile sign; drive uphill to parking area.

Trail Description:

The trail begins out of the old Twentymile Ranger Station area at the end of a short road off Hwy 28. At the gate at the end of the road, first hike 0.5 mile up the Twentymile Trail. Twentymile Creek bubbles merrily along the right side of the wide pathway. After crossing Moore Branch on a sturdy wood bridge, you will see the trail sign for Wolf Ridge on the left at 0.5 mile.

Wolf Ridge Trail climbs steeply for 6.4 miles up on the south range of the Smokies to end at Sheep Pen Gap at the junction of the Gregory Bald Trail. It gains 3,350 feet in its ascent. If you are ambitious and in good shape, you can hike to Parsons Bald near the trail's end, but for an easier walk, you can enjoy simply walking 2 miles up the trail to Campsite #95 as we did.

The hike begins on an old wagon road along Moore Springs Branch, a beautiful creek tumbling down from the higher elevations. There are rushing cascades and spills to enjoy along the creek walk, beautiful foliage in the fall, and wildflowers in abundance in the spring. You will encounter five stream crossings in the first mile on Wolf Ridge Trail. The first is at 0.3 mile on a high

log with a hand rail. The next crossings had similar log bridges at one time, but when we hiked these had rotted out and not been replaced. This meant sitting down to take off your boots, roll up your pants-legs and wading or rock-hopping each crossing. In summer, this would have been more fun than it was in November. None of our hiking books noted the bridges were out. So, plan this hike for warm weather and take a towel!

After the 5th stream crossing, the trail meets the junction of the Twentymile Loop Trail. Many people enjoy turning right on this trail across Long Hungry Ridge to return down the Twentymile Trail in a 7.5 miles loop hike. Continuing on at the junction, Wolf Ridge Trail swings left and rises uphill away from Moore Springs Branch to climb a hill. However, the narrowing pathway soon begins to parallel Dalton Branch on the left. The trail is climbing northwest now between Dalton Ridge below and Wolf Ridge above. This section is a pretty forest walk, although more strenuous and uphill than the first mile of the trail, and you will again meet several stream crossings along the way. After a healthy climb, gaining approximately 1,000 feet of elevation since the Twentymile Loop junction, the trail arrives at Campsite #95, which you will be glad to see at this point. This is a scenic wooded spot for a picnic and a rest before starting your hike back down the mountain.

Dudley Creek Loop Trail

Date Hiked: WINTER - February 11th
Mileage: 6 miles Roundtrip
Our Rating: Moderate
Directions: Hwy 441 into Gatlinburg; left on Hwy 321 at Traffic Light #3; drive approximately 4.5 miles east to Smoky Mountain Riding Stables on the right; park in front of stable gate (stables approximately 1 mile after Traffic Light #3A at Glades Road).

Trail Description:

Dudley Creek Trail is an old hiking trail loop that is now predominantly a horse trail for the Smoky Mountain Riding Stables. Because of this, it is best to hike this trail in the winter when the stable is closed. In summer and heavy tourist seasons, you can still hike on the trail, but you will encounter many inexperienced, hourly riders and a lot of horse piles along the trail. In the winter, hikers have the Dudley Loop Trail all to themselves.

The hike begins at the gated road in front of the stable. Walk up the short drive, thru the stable area past the barn, and then look for the hiking trail that winds to the left alongside the corral fencing. The trail follows the fenceline for a short distance and then winds away from the stable area into the woods below. Within the first half mile there is a rock-hop crossing of shallow Duds Branch. The ongoing trail after the creek is a narrow dirt roadbed that winds gradually up through an open woods. This was an old settlement area in the Smokies and you can see cleared areas where old homes and farms once stood. The trail skirts

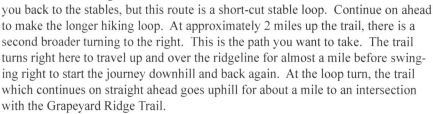

up and down between the woods and a small stream, called Twin Creek, as it works its way up toward Grapeyard Ridge and the Mount Winnesoka peaks above. It's a picturesque area.

As the hike climbs gradually upward, there is a cut-off trail branching right over the creek at about 1 mile. A right turn here will circle and take you back to the stables, but this route is a short-cut stable loop. Continue on ahead to make the longer hiking loop. At approximately 2 miles up the trail, there is a second broader turning to the right. This is the path you want to take. The trail turns right here to travel up and over the ridgeline for almost a mile before swinging right to start the journey downhill and back again. At the loop turn, the trail which continues on straight ahead goes uphill for about a mile to an intersection with the Grapeyard Ridge Trail.

As you cross over the ridgetop on the Dudley Creek Loop trail, look for an open area with a view out over the mountains to Mount Le Conte. This a nice rest spot with a big log to picnic on. After crossing the ridge, the trail swings right to start the downhill journey of the loop. This part of the trail is a relaxing forest walk following along another creek called Little Dudley Creek. This stream is a larger one than Twin Creek and there are some nice tumbling cascades along the trailside before you get back to the trail's end.

Two Mile Loop

Date Hiked: WINTER - March 10th
Mileage: 6+ miles Roundtrip
Our Rating: Strenuous/Moderate
Directions: From Gatlinburg's Traffic Light #10, continue on Hwy 441 1.2 miles to the Sugarlands Riding Stables on the left just before the Sugarlands Visitor Center, turn in the drive and park at the gate.

Trail Description:

The Two Mile Loop combines a network of lovely, little trails just off Hwy 441 near Gatlinburg. Like the Dudley Creek Loop, this loop-trail 2 miles outside of Gatlinburg is used mostly for horses from the Sugarlands Riding Stables, but this is official National Park land and hikers are welcome, too. The best time to hike these trails is when the stable is closed—December to mid March - and early March is a perfect time. The new spring greens are budding out on the

trees, hints of wildflowers are popping up, and you will probably have the quiet trails all to yourself.

After parking at the gate, walk in past the stable and look for the trail leading off to the right to start your hike. There is no official park sign, but the trail is generally known as Two Mile Branch Trail. The open road-bed wanders gradually up the ridgelines below Bullhead Mountain to eventually meet the Sugarlands Trail.

The first section of the hike climbs uphill, rather steeply in spots, through a shady woods and alongside a bubbly little creek called Two Mile Branch. The forest is mostly hardwoods and the way is scenic. At 1 mile, the path crosses an intersection and narrows, moving into a steeper, less scenic section a little rutted out from horse traffic. At 2.1 miles, you pass a cutoff trail on the left. Keep straight here for another half mile or so until you come to a 2nd intersection. Here turn back sharply to the left to start the loop back down.

After a short climb up a ridge, this 3rd section of the trail levels out nicely and you will enjoy some fine mountain vistas as you walk along. The walk leads up and over the ridge and winds in and out of the woods alongside Two Mile Creek until it eventually deadends into a cross trail called Grassy Branch. Turn left here and follow Grassy Branch for a little less than 1 mile. This cut-section will take you back across Two Mile Branch, that you hiked up before, and on down to a right turning onto Twomile Lead. This trail piece winds up and around the ridges and then down to meet and merge with Old Sugarlands Trail above the Little Pigeon River. Follow this relatively flat trail section for about a half mile, being careful to look for the cutoff for the continuing Twomile Lead turning sharply to the right. This last short trail section takes you parallel to Hwy 441 through the lower woods and back to the stables and your car.

Grassy Branch Trail

Date Hiked: WINTER - March 18th
Mileage: 10 miles Roundtrip
Our Rating: Strenuous/Moderate
Directions: Hwy 441 into Gatlinburg to Traffic Light #8; left up Airport Road onto Cherokee Orchard Road to Mynatt Park on right; park and follow LeConte Drive and signs to start of trail
Trail Description:

The Grassy Branch Trail is a very pleasant but little known hiking trail. It wanders in and out of a scenic hardwood forest to climb up the back of Painter Ridge below Bullhead Mountain. The trail begins near Mynatt Park on Chero-

kee Orchard Road behind Gatlinburg. Mynatt Park is a beautiful spot on Le Conte Creek—with picnic tables, a playground, water fountains, and restrooms. Even in heavy tourist seasons, the park is seldom over-crowded and a great place to have a picnic lunch before or after your hike.

From the parking area, walk across the street to the first short street on the left, called LeConte Drive. Walk 0.2 mile down this charming side street with quaint vacation houses on the right side of the street and Le Conte Creek on the left. When the road deadends, swing left on the trail along the creek and follow the path around the last house. Signs here welcome hikers to walk thru to the park. Grassy Branch Trail, which has no beginning trail sign marker, soon swings to the right, away from the creek, to travel into the woods. The trail passes an unmarked side path on the left and then angles right. At approximately 0.5 mile, the trail widens into an old wagon road and moves through a level, open woods of mixed hardwoods and pines. You

200

will pass the remains of a rock wall on the left, the first of many evidences of prior settlements along the trail.

At 0.8 mile, the trail begins to follow along shallow Grassy Branch, a tumbling, gurgly, little stream. The trail rock hops over the stream at 1 mile to swing left and start uphill below a ridgeline. The trail ascends quickly to rise high

above the creek. As the path starts to level out, look for more rock wall foundations in a clearing below the trail.

At 1.4 miles, the path passes around a rocky outcrop, angles uphill, and then begins to follow the stream again, passing through heavy rhododendron and rising to meet a trail intersection with Painter Ridge Trail at approximately 1.6 miles. A park mileage sign stands at the trail junction.

Continue on straight at this intersection through a level wooded section and then up a steep ridge with white quartz along the path. You pass a side trail to the left at 4.2 miles shortly before cresting the ridge top at 4.8 miles. Here there is an open clearing with a rest log and fine views out over the mountain ranges to both sides. We ended our hike 0.2 mile further at the crossing of Two Mile Branch Trail, 5 miles from the start of our hike. If you want to walk another mile, you will intersect Old Sugarlands Trail.

White Oak Branch Trail/

Date Hiked: SPRING - April 14th
Mileage: 8.4 miles Roundtrip
Our Rating: Moderate/Strenuous
Directions: Hwy 441 over mountain to Cherokee, NC; right on Hwy 19 to right at bridge at Bryson City; stay on main road then left onto Lakeview Drive to parking at end of road.

Trail Description:

This was an interesting trail leading out of the end of the "Road to Nowhere" outside Bryson City. After the creation of Fontana Dam, the Federal Government promised a new road along the north shore of the lake, but due to

construction and environmental issues it was never completed. Signs along the road into the National Park show the disappointment of many, announcing: "Welcome to the Road to Nowhere - A Broken Promise."

Access to the Lakeshore Trail begins with a journey through the long rock tunnel at the end of the road. The 1,000 foot tunnel is dark and a little creepy and you might want to bring a flashlight for the walk through it. A Tunnel Bypass Trail, 2.1 miles long, routes around the tunnel but walking through the tunnel saves time and distance. As you walk through, focus your sight on the half-moon light at the end of the tunnel for a forward guide. At the tunnel's end, the roadbed stops abruptly. The Lakeshore Trail ahead is a hard-packed red clay path starting

Lakeshore Trail

out relatively flat, but soon rolling up and down the ridgelines of what locals call Tunnel Ridge. This end of the 16.6 miles Lakeshore Trail was once called The Proctor Trail.

In the first mile of the hike, you pass several turn-offs to your left for other trails, two for the Goldmine Loop Trail that swings down to a campsite on a finger of Fontana Lake and one for the Tunnel Bypass Trail. After the trail junctions are passed, the trail turns right and into a deeper woods, rock-hopping over a shallow stream or two. The largest is Goldmine Branch at 1.5 miles. There were few wildflowers on this trail in April, but we saw a lot of mountain laurel that should be showy in early summer.

At 2.2 miles the trail arrives at an open intersection. Turn right here to start up the White Oak Branch Trail. The narrowing trail ascends through heavy laurel and rhododendron and into a forested area with a softer footing. The path winds up and down around Forney Ridge, dipping down to stream crossings of fingers of

Gray Wolf Creek. After hiking a mile on White Oak, look for an open area in the trail where there used to be a pioneer home. If you poke around here you may find chimney rocks and a spring. There is quartz in this area, too, and you may also find bits of it along the ground.

The last mile of this hike is especially pretty. Near the end of the trail, the path follows along frolicking Whiteoak Branch. There is a rushing cascade here and a scenic crossing of the Branch. This is a great place to have a picnic lunch on the rocks by the stream. The hike ends less than a half mile further up the path, after climbing up around a last ridge and down again to meet Forney Creek and the Forney Creek Trail.

Boogerman Trail

Date Hiked: SPRING - May 28th
Mileage: 7.4 miles Roundtrip
Our Rating: Moderate/Strenuous
Directions: I-40 to NC Exit 20; 0.2 mile to right on Cove Creek Road; follow this gravel road to intersection with paved road; then left and 3 miles to pullover parking on left after the campground.
Trail Description:

The Boogerman Trail is a delightful loop walk up into an un-logged, memorable forest in a quiet part of the Smokies park. Despite its name, Boogerman Trail is neither scarry nor "boogery," and the name of the trail comes from the nickname of an early settler who owned most of the land. You can thank Robert Booger Palmer that most of this area was not heavily cut of its timber. The trailhead starts on the left side of the Cataloochee Road just a few yards past the entrance to the campground.

The hike begins by crossing a 25 foot long, springy log footbridge high up over the rushing Cataloochee Creek below. This is one of the longest

footbridges in the park, and if you have a problem with heights, it will give you a little scare. After crossing the bridge, the trail proceeds for 0.8 mile along Caldwell Fork Trail before starting left up the Boogerman Trail.

The early section of the hike is very pleasurable. Caldwell

Fork Trail follows an old settlers' roadbed through a shady pastoral woodland along a beautiful mountain stream. The Boogerman Trail swings left off of Caldwell Fork at 0.8 mile to loop up Den Ridge, over the upper ridge tops, and down over Horsepen Ridge to meet Caldwell Fork Trail below in a 3.8 miles loop.

Turning at the trail sign, Boogerman Trail first winds its way up through the woods, skirting twice over Dan Branch on the rocks. As the trail rises upward, look for views over the Cataloochee Valley and for large hemlocks and poplars that escaped the loggers' saws. After an early climb, the trail rolls into a more level stretch of pine woods, and then crosses Palmer Branch on a bridge at approximately 2 miles to move into a clearing where Booger Palmer's farm once stood. There is a rock wall here along the trail and, a short distance further along, a huge 6-8 foot diameter tulip tree. All of this upper trail section is very pretty with deep woods, a rhododendron tunnel, and flat, open areas with nice views.

At approximately 2.5 miles, a very steep half-mile climb begins up a section of Horse Pen Ridge to Sag Gap. Mercifully, it is short. From there on the trail is mostly an easy, downhill walk, following along Snake Branch Creek and crossing it four times. The path passes by more rock walls and signs of settlement, including the Carson Messer house and a side spur to the Messer Cemetery, and by a huge tulip poplar with a hollowed out base a person can stand inside of. This is a great place to take a photo. At the

trail's end, you can rest on the logs before starting the 2.8 miles hike back down Caldwell Fork to your car.

Mt. Buckley Trail

Date Hiked: SPRING - June 10th
Mileage: 5.4 miles Roundtrip
Our Rating: Strenuous
Directions: Hwy 441 up Newfound Gap Road to top of mountain; right on Clingmans Dome Road; follow to road's end at Clingmans Dome Parking area.

Trail Description:

Mt. Buckley Trail is a piece of the Appalachian trail heading west from Clingmans Dome on Mt. Love to cross Mt. Buckley and drop down to Double Spring Gap. It walks out across the ridgetops of the state line dividing Tennessee and North Carolina and it is our favorite accessible Appalachian Trail section for ongoing spectacular mountaintop views. So don't miss it! When you plan this hike, please remember that the Clingmans Dome Road to the trailhead is closed in the winter months, from December through March.

We started our hike by walking 0.5 mile on the paved walkway to the Clingmans Dome Tower. It is a short but steep little trail. The walk to the tower

is a poplar one with tourists, and it is always busy. However, Clingmans Dome Tower sits on top of the highest peak in the Smoky Mountains, a point more than 6,640 feet high, so the trudge uphill to see the views is worth it. The tower has a circular walk leading 50 feet up to a railed observation area with a wide panorama of the surrounding mountains. Signs on tower rails point out peaks and cities visible in the distance.

After enjoying the views, look for a marked path north of the tower that leads left onto the Appalachian Trail. This second hiking section wanders through a mountaintop forest of spruce, fir, beech, and ash trees before opening out to intersect the Clingmans Dome Bypass Trail at about 0.5 mile.

Here you may catch a great view back toward Mt. Le Conte before the pathway narrows to begin climbing out on the ridgelines to Mt. Buckley. This hiking section is mostly a steep, downward climb, picking its way over rocks and down rocky stairs on a single-file path. This makes for slow, careful walking and soon increases your pedometer miles. The ridgeline pathway opens out frequently to pass open balds with vistas of the mountain ranges on both sides. There are many points here where you can pause on the grassy heaths to soak in the spectacular scenery.

After a steady drop downhill, the path reaches a low point and then begins a steep march uphill to the top of Mt. Buckley at 6,500 feet to an open area with large rocks and good views. From here on, the trail climbs less strenuously but soon begins a very steep downhill journey on the other side of the mountain to a saddle called Double Spring Gap. This point is about midway between Mt. Buckley and the peaks of Jenkins Knob and Silers Bald. There are many spruce trees in this down-hill section of the hike, as well as more panoramic views out over the mountain ranges. Just before the trail ends at the intersection of Goshen Prong Trail at 2.2 miles, there is a short level section—always a relief on trails of steep ups and downs! For most hikers, this is the point where you will want to turn around. The return hike is as strenuous, or more so, than the hike in. For a short side journey, walk 0.4 mile down Goshen Prong Trail to Double Spring Gap Shelter or for a longer hike continue 1.9 miles more on the Appalachian Trail to Jenkins Knob, along a thin trail pathway called The Narrows, and on to Silers Bald and the intersection of Welch Ridge Trail for an 8.2 miles roundtrip hike.

Tower at Clingmans Dome

207

Hemphill Bald Trail

Date Hiked: SPRING - June 17th
Mileage: 7 miles Roundtrip
Our Rating: Moderate
Directions: I-40 to NC Exit 20; follow Hwy 276 to right on Hwy 19 through Maggie Valley to right at Soco Gap onto Blue Ridge Parkway; take first right on Heintooga Road approximately 3 miles to Polls Gap parking on right.

Trail Description:

Hemphill Bald Trail is one of three hiking trails that begin at the Polls Gap Parking area on the Heintooga Road on Balsam Mountain. To the right of the parking area, look for a trail sign to begin the hike. Hemphill Bald is an 8.5 miles long hiking trail that curls south from its beginning at Polls Gap to swing east to follow along the park boundary. After arriving at an open area called Hemphill Bald at approximately 5 miles, the trail soon angles left down Mc-Clure Ridge to meet Caldwell Fork Trail in the Cataloochee Valley below. At our June hike date, much of the early trail was densely overgrown with grasses, briars, and weeds, often waist high. These slowed our journey and took away from our pleasure in the hike.

In the first mile, Hempbill Bald Trail is flat with only moderate ascents as it curls up through Sugartree Licks and over Whim Knob. The forest is very open and high, the narrow trail choked with weeds, as it climbs from Polls Gap to the park boundary. As you meet Whim Knob at one mile in, the path opens

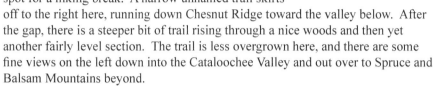

and begins to rise gradually up and over Buck Knob through a mixed hardwood forest. You may see split rail fencelines as you begin to walk along the park boundary line. At Garretts Gap, at 1.7 miles up the trail and just before Buck Knob, there is a nice open site with a rest log on the right side of the trail providing a good spot for a hiking break. A narrow unnamed trail skirts off to the right here, running down Chesnut Ridge toward the valley below. After the gap, there is a steeper bit of trail rising through a nice woods and then yet another fairly level section. The trail is less overgrown here, and there are some fine views on the left down into the Cataloochee Valley and out over to Spruce and Balsam Mountains beyond.

At approximately 2.5 miles, a second un-marked side trail intersects from the right at Maggot Spring Gap. Then the path rises again to begin its climb up to Little Bald Knob at 5,500 feet. This section was the steepest part of our day hike. There are rhododendron in this area and evidence that there would be a wide variety of wildflowers to see in the springtime. At 3 miles, the trail levels out over the top of the Little Bald Knob for about one half mile. We stopped for lunch at another un-marked trail intersection on the bald and turned around at 3.5 miles where the trail begins to drop down toward Pine Tree Gap. If you want to hike further, another 1.2 miles brings you to Hemphill Bald at 5,500 feet, a grassy area 4.7 miles from the trailhead, where settlers once grazed their livestock.

Fork Ridge Trail

Date Hiked: SUMMER - July 7th
Mileage: 6 miles Roundtrip
Our Rating: Moderate/Strenuous
Directions: Hwy 441 up Newfound Gap Road to top of mountain; right on Clingmans Dome Road; 3.5 miles to parking on left side of road at the trailhead.

Trail Description:

Fork Ridge Trail in midsummer is an unexpectedly lush, green adventure walk. It begins at almost 6,000 feet high on top of Mount Collins at Clingmans Dome Road on the top of the Smoky Mountains. Although you would think, as you drive out the Dome road, that all the left-hand trails would drop off as sharply and steeply as a Swiss Alps ski slope, Fork Ridge Trail surprises you. It slips down briefly but then winds out onto the narrow top of the high ridgeline of Fork Ridge, continuing with only a gradual descent.

Start the hike at the park sign and begin this delightful but seldom travelled trail. The first half-mile moves through a mixed hardwood forest of ash, birch, and spruce but then enters a virgin evergreen forest of hemlock, tall red spruce, and young Fraser fir. Watch for a cut-over side trail leading over to the Spruce Fir Nature Trail at 0.2 mile, if you want a side hiking trip.

The footing on the Fork Ridge Trail is soft with layers of pine needles beneath your hiking boots, and you will find many small, tight-scaled pinecones along the pathway. Vast evergreens tower overhead, and both sides of the trail are bordered with thick sweeps of lacy fern and green mosses underneath the tall

trees. There were still some wildflowers and rhododendron on our July hike, and occasionally there were rocky outcrops on the sides of the trail, with multi-colored layers mixed with quartz. Many of the trees here on Fork Ridge are truly large in diameter, and some soar so high into the sky that you have to tilt your head back just to see to the top of them.

At approximately 1.5 miles, the trail angles sharply right for a half-mile before angling back left in a U-shape to continue its downward descent. You will not make quick walking time on Fork Ridge as you hike. The trail is very narrow with roots and rocks to pick your way over on the narrow ridgetops of the mountain. To the left side of the path, the trail often hangs on sheer drop-offs and you must walk with care. In several spots, you hike across wet trickles and seeps, and at about 2 miles the trail crosses a small stream, probably a part of Peg Divide Branch. Large red spruce and yellow birch trees grow in this trail section.

At 2.5 miles, the downhill slope of the trail steepens, moving through a forest of huge hemlock trees, many 5 feet in circumference. It is a treat to travel through an old growth forest like this, but keep an eye on your pedometer miles, and don't get carried away with the ease of the trail's descent. The return is all uphill and strenuous. We turned around for our journey back at approximately 3 miles, and it was a rather strenuous uphill return.

Many trails are also enjoyed by horseback users.

Chestnut Branch Trail

Date Hiked: FALL - September 22nd
Mileage: 4 miles Roundtrip
Our Rating: Strenuous
Directions: I-40 E to Exit 451 at Waterville; follow signs 3 miles toward Big Creek Campground but stop at Ranger Station to park just before trailhead.

Trail Description:

Chestnut Branch Trail is on the right side of the gravel road that travels in to Big Creek Campground. The trail is less than a half mile past the intersection of Hwy 32, coming in to the right from Cosby, and you can reach this trailhead and Big Creek Campground and other trails in this area by alternately driving in from Cosby on this winding two-lane road.

The Chestnut Branch Trail is a 2 miles hike climbing steeply to the Mt. Cammerer Ridge and the Appalachian Trail. The early part of the trail first climbs up Buck Ridge along the right of Chestnut Branch stream. The trail does not always follow close beside the stream, but you can usually hear it tumbling along back through the woods. The trail is relatively narrow, single file, and rocky on the lower section, the way shady, moist, and sometimes muddy through the deep woods. This is a good environment for mushrooms, and we saw many varieties of these on our September hike.

The first half-mile of the trail travels upward in a steady climb through a forest of hardwoods, evergreens, and rhododendron. Near the half mile point watch for a clearing after crossing a little side creek. This was the site of an old pioneer homesite and you will see remnants of its rock walls and some rusted

out artifacts as you pass. Nine families once lived in this rough mountain area. Beyond this point, the trail swings back to follow the creekside of Chestnut Branch. You will enjoy several scenic spots along the streamside as you climb, where multiple cascades roll over mossy rocks. At the first switchback, the trail climbs very sharply to the right up a ridge, curling finally left to a second sharp switchback before straightening out again to finish its ascent up to the Mt. Cammerer ridgetops.

As the trail nears the 1.5 miles mark, it crosses the stream and travels though an area thick with rhododendron. You rock-hop over the water here and will cross the same stream several more times as you climb upward, rising through a cove of tulip trees on the side of Mt. Cammerer Ridge. Chestnut Branch is nearing its headwaters as the trail rises and the upper creek crossings are not deep. We were hiking after recent rains, but in a drier season, some of these crossings might be mere rivulets. The last half mile of the trail is the steepest and the hardest, rising almost 1,000 feet in a short distance. This makes a 2 miles hike feel like 4, and it also makes the downhill return a strenuous walk as well. From the trail's end, it is 1.1 miles to the Davenport Gap Shelter and 1.9 miles to Davenport Gap.

A variety of colorful mushrooms can be found along most trails

Lewellyn Cove Loop

Date Hiked: FALL - September 29th
Mileage: 4 miles Roundtrip
Our Rating: Moderate
Directions: Hwy 321 from Maryville to right on Foothills Parkway; left at end of Parkway on Hwy 129 and over mountain to Hwy 28; trailhead 1 mile past Fontana Village Registration.
Trail Description:

Combining Lewellyn Cove Loop and Lewellyn Nature Trail provides a great hike just outside the Smokies boundary in the Fontana, North Carolina

area. The trailhead is on the right side of Hwy 28 between the entrances to Fontana Village and the road to Fontana Dam. You will see a huge wood sign at the parking lot announcing the trail entrance. At approximately 1.5 miles further up the road, after the entrance to Fontana Dam, the Appalachian Trail crosses over Hwy 28, making this an area popular with hikers.

To begin your hike on Lewellyn Cove Loop, follow the Lewellyn Nature Trail up a series of wood steps and then uphill. The trail begins by ascending gradually over the side of Bee Cove Knob below the Yellow Creek Mountains. After a climb up and around a scenic ridgeline through the woods, the path comes to a split of the Loop Trail and the shorter Nature Trail. Continue left as Lewellyn Cove Loop continues climbing uphill, often steeply, through a fine, mixed hardwood forest. After several swichbacks, the loop trail meets a side trail coming in from the left at approximately 1 mile. This unmarked trail leads east over the ridge to meet the Appalachian Trail before it starts its climb up into the Nantahala Forest. Unlesss you want to explore a little of this side trail, stay to the right to continue on Lewellyn Cove Loop.

After the 1 mile intersection, the Loop trail rolls gradually right to start across a more level upper ridgeline. Any steep uphill climbing is over now, and the rest of the 3 miles hike will have only undulating ups and downs. The trail grows less rocky now, and softer underfoot, and you can stretch out your stride on a delightful shady forest path with varied trees, mosses, mushrooms, and wildflowers. Watch for a beautiful vista out to Fontana Dam on the right at 1.5 miles before the loop trail turns right to start its return. On the downhill hike, you will rock-hop two small streams at 2 miles and 2.5 miles. At 3 miles, the trail arrives at an open area where a broad pathway leads in from Fontana Village. Stay to the right here following the Loop trail on through a stretch of open woods soon paralleling Hwy 28 below. The trail crosses two log bridges over pretty creek branches in this section before coming to the end of the hike. This is a nice trail to walk in any season. It is known for its wildflowers in the spring and for its rich fall foliage of reds, yellows, and oranges in the fall. Be sure to enjoy it when you are in the Fontana area.

Gregory Bald Trail

Date Hiked: FALL - October 26th
Mileage: 6 miles Roundtrip
Our Rating: Moderate/Strenuous
Directions: Hwy 321 to Townsend Wye; right on Laurel Creek Road to its end into Cades Cove Loop; right on Forge Creek to right on Parson Branch 3.2 miles to parking.
Trail Description:

    This is a beautiful and memorable trail that weaves in and out along the ridgelines of Hannah Mountain as it rises up to Gregory Bald high on the mountaintop. The bald is a 15-acre grassy meadow 4,000 feet high with out-standing views of the mountain ranges in all directions. Mid June is a favorite time to hike to the bald as there are hundreds of azaleas in bloom then, including red-orange flame azaleas. In October, when we hiked, spectacular views of fall foliage abound. We hiked up 3 miles to Panther Gap for a 6-miles walk to enjoy the fall leaves but did not hike to the bald that day. There are two important time factors to consider when planning a hike on the Gregory Bald Trail. The first is the time it takes to drive through the slow traffic in Cades Cove, and the second is the time it takes to drive out one-way Parson Branch and back around the mountain on Hwy 129 after your hike is over.

    The trail begins by curling south out of Sams Gap at the parking area pull-over on Parson Branch Road. The single-file trail angles south to begin its

journey up Long Hungry Ridge. There are tulip poplars, oak, and other richly colored hardwoods in the open forest you hike through. The trail switches right at approximately 0.5 mile to coil around a ridgeline and then swings back left again. As the trail rises, there are more and more panoramic views back over Cades Cove and toward North Carolina. The first two miles pose only a gradual ascent and a moderate hike. The trail winds up through hardwoods, pines, hemlocks, laurel, and rhododendron on a narrow trail with a predominantly soft underfooting. The path drops slightly through a gap at approximately 1.5 miles, ascends again, and then passes through an open, rocky ravine at approximately 1.8 miles. Look for an especially large poplar tree with a broad diameter just after this point. It is on the right side of the trail.

At 2 miles, the trail angles steeply upward and begins to climb more strenuously. The trail rises for 0.5 mile along a steep slope to arrive at an open vista point before it curls up and around the ridgeline again. You can see back to the cove here and out over the mountain ranges. Soon the trail turns left toward Panther Gap, but you will still find points where the trail opens to more fine views. You will know when you arrive at Panther Gap because the trail switches back sharply right before beginning to climb again to Sheep Pen Gap and Campsite #13 at 4 miles and then on to the bald at 4.5 miles.

Goshen Prong Trail

Date Hiked: SPRING - April 21st

Mileage: 12.4 miles Roundtrip

Our Rating: Moderate

Directions: Hwy 321 to Townsend Wye; left on Little River Road to right into Elkmont; left up side road just before campground to parking area.

Trail Description:

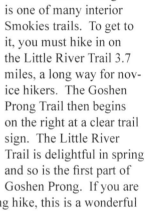

Goshen Prong is one of many interior Smokies trails. To get to it, you must hike in on the Little River Trail 3.7 miles, a long way for novice hikers. The Goshen Prong Trail then begins on the right at a clear trail sign. The Little River Trail is delightful in spring and so is the first part of Goshen Prong. If you are up for a long hike, this is a wonderful one to take.

A full description of the Little River Trail is in an earlier part of this book (pages 16-17). This early section of the trail follows a gradually ascending roadbed directly alongside Little River, a tumbling mountain stream full of falls and cascades. It's a favorite trail in spring for its many wildflowers, including several varieties of trillium. At 1.3 miles, you pass the intersection to Cucumber Gap Trail and at 1.7 another to Huskey Gap Trail after crossing Little River on a broad bridge. The trail narrows now, with Little River running on the right. At 2.7 miles, the path arrives at a broad, open intersection where you can stop to rest on a big boulder before turning right on the Goshen Prong Trail. After a short walk, the trail crosses over Little River on a long, log footbridge. Then it meanders up an unexpectedly picturesque open valley on an old wagon road. There is even still grass growing between the wagon ruts. In April an abundance of wildflowers are along the way including white foamflower, geraniums, trillium, wild purple phlox, and showy orchis.

At approximately 0.5 mile, the trail moves closer to Fish Camp Prong, a rushing mountain creek coming down from the high mountains. Soon the walk narrows to a single-file footpath, following the creekside for over 3.3 miles to Campsite #33. The walk is pleasant on this trail section, with only a gradual ascent. It moves through a little hidden valley with mountains on both sides as it winds along the stream-side.

After the first mile, you will see a big cascade on the right, sliding over the rocks. Further up the trail are more cascades, slides, and spills, many falling into beautiful green pools below. Be sure to watch for one waterfall which drops down for about 5 feet into a deep pool below it. There is also a high rock ledge on the left of the trail to look for that is covered in woods plants and wildflowers. It is hard to decide when to turn around on Goshen Prong, all of the trail is so pretty, but we did so at approximately 2.5 miles up the trail, still bringing our overall hike to more than 12 miles.

Long Bunk Trail

Date Hiked: SPRING - May 5th
Mileage: 7.4 miles Roundtrip
Our Rating: Strenuous
Directions: I-40 to NC Exit 20; 0.2 mile to right on Cove Creek Road; up this gravel road approximately 5.8 miles to Cove Creek Gap at top of mountain; trail on right with pull-over parking.
Trail Description:

Reaching the trailhead of the Long Bunk Trail involves taking a slow, bumpy drive up a dirt and gravel road, called NC Route 284, for 5.5 miles. You travel this stretch of rough road after already driving in over the winding unpaved Cove Creek Road leading into the Cataloochee valley. After parking at the trailhead, you must then hike in one mile on Little Cataloochee Trail to reach Long Bunk. Little Cataloochee is a valley trail with rolling ups and downs. It ascends sharply from the road, winds across a creek, and then angles up and around a ridge to meet Long Bunk Trail on the right. Perhaps the signpost here, saying: "6 miles to Mt. Sterling" should be a warning that climbs are ahead on Long Bunk, since Mt. Sterling is the highest peak in the area.

As you begin the Long Bunk Trail, the path soon becomes a steep one as it travels up a settlers' wagon route through a predominantly hardwood forest. The old roadbed is rough and rocky and the walking is hard, as you must pick your way over and around the rocks. At 0.2 mile on the right side of the path is the fenced Hannah Cemetery with pioneer graves. Stop here for a rest and to walk through the cemetery. There are around 50 graves and many have

LONG BUNK TRAIL

Great Smoky Mtns

headstones you can read the pioneer names on. The trail continues its ascent through the woods after the cemetery. We saw wild, purple geranium and many lacy, green ferns as we climbed. Just after the half-mile point, the trail drops into a small open valley where settlers once lived. There is a creek here which mingles with the trail for a stretch. You may see remains of an old log cabin foundation to the right of the trail.

The trail then begins to climb again, quite steeply in spots, before dropping and coming to an easy crossing of Dude Branch creek near 1.5 miles. The path narrows somewhat as you hike on, but becomes steeper as it continues upward through the woods to a more level crest at 3 miles up the trail. The forest here has become denser and there are some huge oak trees here, a few as much as 5 feet in diameter. A short distance further, the trail comes to its first scenic area at a crossing of Correll Branch. Another crossing soon follows, and then the trail ends in less than a half mile further at Mt. Sterling Gap and an intersection with the Mt. Sterling Trail at 3.7 miles. We had our picnic on this upper section of the trail by the stream before turning back for our return. The downhill walk back was easier than the hike in.

Noland Divide Trail

Date Hiked: SPRING - May 12th
Mileage: 6.6 miles Roundtrip
Our Rating: Moderate
Directions: Hwy 441 up Newfound Gap Road to top of mountain; right on Clingmans Dome Road; drive 5.5 miles to trailhead and parking area on left side of the road.
Trail Description:

As you drive out Clingmans Dome Road and look left down the steep drop offs on the mountainside, you'd never guess that the Noland Divide Trail would lead you out on a delightful ridgeline walk instead of down a plummeting mountain slope. However, the Noland Divide Trail, somewhat like Fork Ridge Trail, slips down from the road and then walks out along a high Smokies ridge.

The trail begins at a gate and follows, at first, steeply down through an open hardwood forest for 0.5 mile to a rain-monitoring tower. The path then veers around the tower and downhill to an intersection. The jeep road continues ahead right, while Noland Divide turns left at the sign onto a narrower trail. After a further drop, the path levels to only a gradual descent. The Noland Divide Trail now begins walking out onto a southeast ridgeline 5,000 feet high with Deep Creek basin far below to the left and Noland Creek far down to the right. This section of the trail is especially beautiful. It wanders through a lush, moist woods that receives heavy rainfall. Never logged, the virgin forest contains towering red spruce, Fraser fir, and hemlocks, mixed with yellow birch, oaks, and other hardwoods. The forest floor is thick with fern and full of wildflowers

in the spring. Clintonia yellow corn-lily, or bluebeard, are profuse with their shiny green leaves and white flowers. We had never seen so much corn-lily in one place on the trails. There were also delicate bluets clustered in colorful masses along the way and, at these higher elevations, we still saw painted trillium and red trillium just beginning to bloom in mid May.

After the first half mile, the trail swings left and around Roundtop Knob. Gradually, the forest changes from one of tall spruce and evergreens to one thick with hardwoods. As the trail reaches 1.5 miles, watch for the first impressive views to the left. Others soon follow as the pathway opens out at several other points. At 2 miles, Noland Divide moves through rhododendron tunnels and passes by several logs you can stop to rest or picnic on before beginning a slightly steeper descent for approximately a half mile. At 2.7 miles, the trail levels out again with panoramic vistas to the right of Forney Ridge. Just after 3 miles, the ongoing pathway passes over a knob and starts downhill through rhododendron and laurel toward Sassafras Gap and a junction with Pole Road Creek Trail at 3.8 miles. Remember that the return hike is uphill on this hike and a little more strenuous. We turned around at about 3.3 miles to start back, a half mile before the junction.

Smokemont Loop Trail

Date Hiked: SPRING - May 19th
Mileage: 6.6 miles Roundtrip
Our Rating: Strenuous
Directions: Hwy 441 over Newfound Gap and down the mountain to Smokemont Campground; turn left after bridge and drive to back of campground to park.
Trail Description:

Smokemont Loop Trail is a "Bear Went Over the Mountain" trail rolling up out of the south end of the campground to come back down at the north end. It rises up to climb Richland Mountain to a height of 3,684 feet and then

back down again. The steep rises up and down make this trail a strenuous little hike. Trail signs say the loop is 5.6 miles, but forget to add the 1-mile walk between the trail ends of the loop as part of the overall trail mileage.

We parked at the far north end of the Smokemont Campground and walked back 1 mile to the south end to hike the trail clockwise, starting at the concrete bridge over Bradley Creek at the Smokemont trail sign. The trail first follows 0.2 mile up a roadbed and then branches right on a soft, narrow footpath that will weave in and out and up the backside of the mountain. Look for a trail to the left in this lower section that leads over to the Bradley cemetery. There you will find old graves dating back to the 1800s.

Once you start uphill on the backside of the Richland Mountain, the ascent is continually steep and will rise 1,400 feet in 2.5 miles. It switches to the

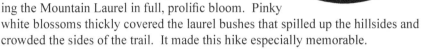

right and left up the ridgelines with deep drop offs to the left. As you climb, you will see a finger creek of the Oconaluftee River below and, later, will cross that creek and several seeps as you make your way upward. Although the climb on this section is strenuous, hiking in mid May offered us the special pleasure of finding the Mountain Laurel in full, prolific bloom. Pinky white blossoms thickly covered the laurel bushes that spilled up the hillsides and crowded the sides of the trail. It made this hike especially memorable.

At 2.5 miles from the start of the trailhead, the trail comes to an open knob at the top of Richland Mountain. The path winds around the knob and then starts a descent downhill to Bradley Creek below. The first mile downhill passes through a high, dry, open forest. The trail is a dirt path, narrow, and often very steep. Toward the end of the descent, the trail moves into a more picturesque woodland along Bradley Fork Creek. At the end of the downhill pathway, the trail crosses over the rushing mountain stream on a long, high, bouncy footlog that may have you hanging to the handrail! The last 1.7 miles of the loop hike follows to the right down Bradley Fork Trail and back to the campground on a broad, open streamside roadbed. You can stretch out your legs and enjoy the shady trees, flat path, and scenic cascades in the creek as you hike. At the end of the Bradley Fork Trail, follow the campground road to the right back to your car.

Whiteoak Sink

Date Hiked: WINTER - Mar 6th
Mileage: 7 miles Roundtrip
Our Rating: Moderate
Directions: Hwy 321 to Townsend Wye; right on Laurel Creek Road; drive 3.9 miles to the parking lot on right of road at School-house Gap trailhead.

Trail Description:

The trail to Whiteoak Sink winds its way to an area filled with geological wonders: sinks, limestone caverns, and a waterfall that drops over a limestone bluff to disappear into a cave. This hike is a well-known one to area residents and hiking clubs, but it is not written up in any of the Smoky Mountain trail guide books. The reason for this may be because the trail is not marked by the park service or because there are caves in the sink area that are dangerous to the public. If you hike the Whiteoak Sink trail, be sure to follow the trail directions, as there are no park signs or trail markers and there are many side trails that might mislead you along the way.

Begin the hike by walking 1.2 miles up Schoolhouse Gap Trail to Dorsey Gap where you will see the Turkeypen Ridge Trail on the left. A few yards

Whiteoak Sink Falls

further on, watch for an unmarked trail dropping down to the left. This is the start of the walk to the Whiteoak Sink. The trail descends gradually downhill to a shallow rill crossing and then through rhododendron tunnels to come out into a rolling, green valley beween two high hills—Scott Mountain on the right and Turkeypen ridge on the left. Here, the path soon walks alongside a shallow stream on the left. Watch for a turning of the trail over a low, boggy crossing of this stream at about a half mile from the start of the sink trail. It is easy to miss. Find a route over the creek here and pick up the path again on the other side. Once across, the onward trail is easy to see and follow. It soon crosses a 2nd shallow stream, and then angles right to begin climbing up a ridge. The trail will wind over this ridge and across

another before dropping steeply downhill at 2.5 miles into the Whiteoak Sink area which is aproximately 1/2 mile long and a quarter mile wide. The sinks are large depressions caused by collapses of the ground into underlying caverns below, created long years ago as the mountains were forming. You will see the first sink to the left of the trail and soon another on the right. Vertical limestone bluffs rise up to 80 feet around the sink area and, if you look carefully, you may see "windows" or holes through the west edge of the rock wall.

After passing the 2nd sink, the trail moves downhill through the woods to come out into another open valley. The trail splits here. Take the right trail to reach Whiteoak Sink Falls, about 0.5 mile from the sink area. A small stream drops 40 feet over limestone bluffs to create a long cascade of falling water and then disappears into a cave below. The stream simply vanishes like water going down a sink! It is a fine spot for a picnic on fallen trees beside the falls.

After seeing the falls, return down the same route, remembering to turn left up the hill again for a 6 miles roundtrip hike back to your car. To see two more caves and another sink, adding another mile to your roundtrip hike, continue on the trail past the intersection. You will soon see the entrance to the Blowhole Cave on your right at the base of a rocky bluff. The cave is protected by a metal cage over the opening.

A trail to the right of the Blowhole leads a few yards to an unmarked trail that climbs up the ravine approximately 0.5 mile to a third sink. Down inside this sink is the entrance to the Scott Mountain Cave. If you walk closer to look into the cave, you can hear the sounds of a stream from deep inside the limestone cavern. All caves in the sinks area are dangerous and should only be entered with permission of the parks department—so don't try to go inside any of them! It is a memorable enough day to see all these interesting sights on your hiking adventure.

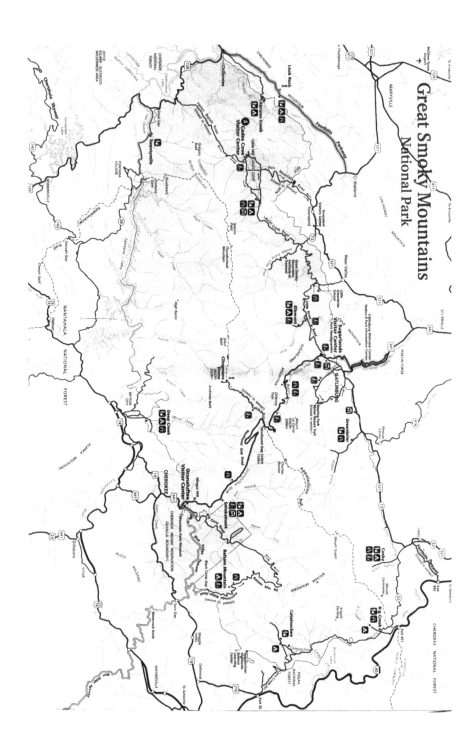

ALPHABETICAL TRAIL INDEX

Trail Index by Regions

Hoarfrost - an icy wonder when fog freezes on the mountaintop.

Trail Index by Regions

The Mountains constantly call: come experience, come explore, come enjoy!

HIKING TIPS

1. CARRY A HIKING MAP. Hiking trail maps can be obtained at visitor centers and hiking shops in the area and are inexpensive. One of the best and least expensive is the National Park Service's map called "Great Smoky Mountains Trail Map." A common misconception with new hikers is that you can't get lost when hiking a single trail. Most trails intersect with other trails, and although there are trail signs, you can still get disoriented on a return hike and take a wrong turn. A hiking map will always be the surest way to prevent taking wrong turns and adding extra travel.

2. PACK LIGHT, BUT PACK RIGHT. Carry all the essential items you need, but any extra weight you pack will get heavier as you hike. Always carry water as even in cold weather you can get dehydrated on strenuous trails. High energy snacks (nuts, dried fruit, trailmix, etc.) and a light sandwich can give you an extra boost and make the hike more enjoyable. We also recommend a light plastic rain poncho—weather can change quickly in the mountains and it's important to stay dry to prevent hypothermia. A compass, belt snap-on mileage meter, tissue pack, small first aid kit with band aids (blisters are common with novice hikers), and compact inflatable cushion or small towel to sit on are items you should carry. A lightweight back pack for longer hikes or a "fanny pack" for shorter hikes will carry the essential items.

3. GOOD HIKING BOOTS ARE ESSENTIAL An investment in good quality hiking boots or shoes is the best single item for quality hiking. Trails can be rocky and rough at times and your feet take the most wear. Nothing can ruin a nice hike quicker than blistered or injured feet or ankles due to shoddy footwear.

4. DRESS IN LAYERS IN COLD WEATHER. It is better to dress in layers on cold-weather hikes. The most important thing is to peel off layers if you find yourself getting overheated on a hike. Sweating must be avoided even in winter because the wet clothing can cause chilling and severe discomfort when you start cooling off.

5. STAY ON THE HIKING TRAILS. Every year hikers get lost when leaving the marked trails. The varied topography of the mountains makes it easy to get disoriented and confused as to direction. It may look like fun to take a "short-cut" or explore off the trails but this can lead to dangerous situations. There's plenty to enjoy on the marked trails, so stay on the trail!

6. BE A GOOD STEWARD OF THE LAND. Take plastic bags with you and carry out all your trash—leave the mountains as clean as you found them so that others can enjoy the beauty of nature, too.

About The Authors

J.L. Stepp is a native East Tennessean who lives in Knoxville, Tennessee. Stepp owns and operates S & S Communications, established in 1990, which publishes a monthly outdoor magazine called *Tennessee Fishing & Hunting Guide*. The magazine covers fishing and hunting topics in Tennessee and is distributed in print form to advertisers at the first of every month. The magazine can also be downloaded from the internet by going to *www. tnfhg.com*. J.L., a graduate of The University of Tennessee, also markets UT Vols sports related products such as football and basketball schedules, limited edition prints, and licensed sports collectibles. Stepp's background includes over 45 years in sales, marketing, management, and publications. He enjoys a wide variety of outdoor sports, including golf, fishing, and hiking.

Lin Stepp, also a native Tennessean, works as both a businesswoman and an educator. She is on adjunct faculty at Tusculum College, where she teaches research, and at King University, where she teaches a variety of psychology and counseling courses. Her business background includes over 25 years in marketing, sales, production art, and regional publishing. She has editorial and writing experience in regional magazines and in the academic field. Stepp has five published works, each set in different locations around the Smoky Mountains. Her next Smokies novels, including *Down by the River*, *Makin' Miracles*, and *Saving Laurel Springs* will be released by Kensington Publishing in 2014 and 2015. Previous titles include: *Second Hand Rose* (2013), *Delia's Place* (2012), *For Six Good Reasons* (2011), *Tell Me About Orchard Hollow* (2010), and *The Foster Girls* (2009). For more about Stepp's fictional work see: *www.linstepp.com*.